Five Things I Wish They'd Told Me When I Became a Christian

Five Things I Wish They'd Told Me When I Became a Christian

Rob Frost

Authentic

12 11 10 09 08 07 06   7 6 5 4 3 2 1

First published 2006 by Authentic Media
9 Holdom Avenue, Bletchley, Milton Keynes, Bucks,
MK1 1QR, UK
and 129 Mobilization Drive, Waynesboro, GA 30830-4575, USA
www.authenticmedia.co.uk
Authentic Media is a division of Send the Light Ltd, a company limited
by guarantee (registered charity no. 270162)

British Library Cataloguing in Publication Data

A catalogue record for this book is available from the
British Library

ISBN 1-85078-670-4

Cover design by fourninezero design.
Print Management by Adare Carwin
Typeset by GCS, Leighton Buzzard
Printed in Great Britain by J.H. Haynes and Co., Sparkford

Contents

Introduction

Why five?

I've come to that stage in life where there's more in the past than there's likely to be in the future! It's a sobering time of life, and I'm fascinated to see how my priorities have changed in comparison with the list of things I thought were important twenty or thirty years ago. I guess this is part of the natural flow of life, and something which comes to us all with the passing of the years.

This stage of life is also time for a little retrospection, and for seeing some of my earlier experiences with the clarity and perspective which only a bit of hindsight can bring. I certainly don't have any regrets about the way my life has panned out. Far from it: I'm filled with gratitude to God, whose grace and love have done more in me and for me than I could ever have hoped was possible.

As I look back, however, I can see that it took longer to learn some lessons than it should have done. I can also identify some of the things I should have been taught from the outset of my Christian journey, but which, for one reason or another, I was never told or wasn't mature enough to hear. Unfortunately, there are many of them!

This book started out as 'Fifty things I wish I'd been told', but even then I had done some initial editing.

(I think the list was originally seventy-five!) When I began to write, however, it quickly became clear to me that the five things outlined in this book were the most difficult problem areas that I have struggled with in my faith. These were the five areas which caused me most pain, the five unresolved issues which could have been most damaging to my faith.

Strangely enough, as I began to write, many of the other forty-five areas seemed to merge into these five. In the end, a number of the original items on my agenda have found their way into this book anyway, so I'm not planning on writing another ten books like this!

This material is not just written for young people who are starting out on the road of discipleship. It's also for those who are at later stages of faith but who may like to visit these areas and to see how they have struggled with them too.

Some of the material here has appeared in different forms down the years, but much of it is new. It is all intensely personal, and it is written straight from the heart. This book isn't so much a theological exploration of the areas outlined, but more a personal account of one man's struggle to deal with some of the things which could have wrecked his faith.

And what do I hope will result from all these hours of hammering away at my laptop in airport lounges, hotel rooms and the back seats of cars whilst travelling around the world? Two things. First, that some younger Christian will be spared some of the struggle I've gone through in coming to terms with my faith. Secondly, that all of us Christians might give more time to mentoring, discipling and encouraging the rising generation who are following us along this amazing road to the cross.

Rob Frost
Devon, October 2005

Also by Rob Frost

Devotional/theological books

Break Me, Shape Me, Marshall Pickering, 1986
Breaking Bread, Kingsway, 1988
Pilgrims, Kingsway, 1990
When I Can't Pray, Kingsway, 1995
Which Way for the Church? Kingsway, 1997
Thinking Clearly About Science, Monarch, 1998
A New Start, Hodder, 1999
Sharing Jesus in a New Millennium, Scripture Union, 2000
Jesus for the Third Millennium, Bible Reading Fellowship, 2000
A Closer Look at New Age Spirituality, Kingsway, 2001
Here & Now, CWR, 2002
Destiny, Authentic Media, 2004
Essence, Kingsway, 2003
A Journey Through Advent, CWR, 2004
Kids @ Essence, Kingsway, 2004
Evangelism in a Spiritual Age, Church House Publishing, 2005
Freedom Fighters, Authentic Media, 2005
The Way of the Cross, CWR, 2006
Five Things I Wish They'd Told Me, Authentic Media, 2006

Novels

Gospel End, Kingsway, 1991
Broken Cross, Monarch, 1992
Burning Questions, Monarch, 1994
Hopes and Dreams, Monarch, 1999

1

What they didn't tell me about believing

My personal journey

Looking back across the years, I am amazed at how little I really understood about Christian believing when I first became a Christian. I'm staggered at just how little the more mature Christians around me taught me about the ancient creeds and the transforming power of salvation. For years I struggled because I had a flawed understanding of the basis of my faith and what it really means to believe in Christ and to 'be saved'.

When I was a few months old my mother used to take me on her preaching engagements and she would place my carrycot behind the pulpit. Apparently, when I cried she would rock it by lifting her foot in the handle, in the hope that I might go to sleep during the sermon. I am deeply grateful for the Christian home in which I was reared, for the daily prayers at my bedside, and for the encouragement to serve the Lord which my parents constantly gave me.

By the time I was a teenager, however, I was bored and fed up with church life, and I preferred riding my bike around the park to being in Sunday school. I had been taken to church since my earliest childhood days, and I'd had enough of it all.

My cherished memories of Sunday school were of the pranks I played rather than the lessons I learnt. I remember being told to stand in the corridor for 'mucking around' during the Lord's prayer, and I got into trouble in the senior group for tying a girl's hair to the back of a chair.

By my mid-teens I thought I knew everything about Christianity, but I didn't know Jesus for myself. I had been to so many church meetings that I knew a lot of Bible teaching, but I didn't have a personal experience of Christ myself.

One weekend our youth group went on a camp to a village called Alvechurch, just outside Birmingham. It was then that I began to see beyond my Sunday school religion. At a barbecue one night our leader challenged us to consider just one miracle, that God loved the world so much that he visited the planet in the person of Jesus.

I went for a walk alone, and in the woodland clearing I looked up to see a great panoply of stars stretching into distant space. In the quiet of that night I prayed, 'I'm not sure if I can accept it all or believe it all, Lord, but if you are real, be real to me.'

That moment of openness was the beginning of my journey to salvation. Over the following year I struggled with many aspects of the Christian faith. I struggled to accept that Jesus existed as a real person, but I read up on history and began to discover that there was evidence for Christ's life and ministry in the writings of early Jewish historians such as Josephus.

At the teenage discussion group I went to, I started out as the argumentative sceptic but gradually began to realize that Jesus was far more than just a 'nice guy'. The more I discovered about him, the more I wanted to know him in a real way for myself.

I remember a statement that had a special impact on me at this time. I read that Oxford don C.S. Lewis had declared, 'Either this man was the Son of God, or else a madman or something worse.' So I began to wrestle with this 'either/or' scenario.

I came to see that no one throughout history could be compared with him, for the effect of his life on individuals and on nations had been immeasurable. Here was someone who not only preached forgiveness, but who hung on a cross to prove it.

I slowly came to understand what Swiss theologian Karl Barth said when he was asked what he thought was the most profound concept in Christianity. He simply replied, 'Jesus loves me, this I know, for the Bible tells me so.'

My Christian friends convinced me to take Jesus seriously, and to search for him with all my heart. As I met more and more young believers, I began to want the kind of relationship with Jesus which they so obviously had. I wanted to know the kind of love which Cliff Richard said was 'the most radical, urgent and relevant piece of Good News ever to be delivered,' and about which he added, 'Personally, I am as convinced about the truth of it as I am about anything.'

I knew that my intellectual assent to Jesus was not enough. I had never really put my faith in him. Things came to a head when I went back to the youth camp at Alvechurch the following Easter. On Easter Sunday morning I heard a very elderly deaconess preach about the risen Jesus, and the story of the Resurrection suddenly made sense to me.

After lunch I took time out from the rest of the group and went for a walk in the woods. I found the same place where I had prayed before, but this time I prayed, 'Lord, I give you my life. All that I am, and all

I ever hope to be.' I knelt and asked Jesus Christ to be my personal Friend and Saviour.

For the first time I believed in the reality of the living Christ who had died for me and who could enter my life in a new and powerful way. I did not have a dramatic conversion experience, just a new sense of peace and closeness to Jesus. Before this, Jesus had seemed far away, high up – as if on the mountain top. He was distant and unknowable, and I couldn't even reach him in prayer.

But when I came to know Jesus for myself in the stillness of the forest that Easter, he came down from the mountain top to walk by my side. He became my personal Friend – always there to share whatever joys or sorrows might come my way. For the first time I believed his great promise: 'I will never leave you nor forsake you.' I took him at his word.

Soon afterwards I stuck a sign on my bedroom door which read, 'Tell Jesus.' Whenever I went out of the door I couldn't help but see it. Sometimes I would go out to sit an exam, enduring that awful nerve-racking feeling that precedes university papers. As I went out of the door the sign reminded me to 'tell Jesus'.

At other times I would go out feeling great as I set off to meet my girlfriend. The sign reminded me that in every situation Jesus was there to share my life with me. I discovered that knowing Jesus is at the heart of real Christianity.

Where did my faith really begin? Was it in some of those early Sunday school experiences when, despite my general lack of interest, there were special moments of knowing his presence? Was it when I first came to love Jesus, and gave my life to him? Or did it start in the earliest days of my childhood, when I glimpsed something of the life of faith in my parents? I really don't know, but as I look back it seems that the whole process of becoming a Christian was about a growing revelation of his presence which unfolded from my earliest experiences and which has continued through every phase of my life.

Many of us find our way into Christian faith through discovering a living relationship with Jesus. Many evangelists frame their challenge as 'giving your life to Jesus' or 'becoming a friend of Jesus' or even 'falling in love with Jesus'.

This is a good starting point for Christian discipleship, but I fear that countless new believers have been stunted in their Christian growth because they did not move beyond this first step on the journey. They never received a proper grounding in what Christian salvation really is. That was certainly true for me.

I've come to see that there is much more to Christianity than just 'finding a friend in Jesus'. I wish that someone had taught me about the rich truths of salvation from the very start.

Salvation

It wasn't very culturally acceptable in the denomination in which I was discipled to talk about being 'saved' or 'rescued'. I was taught that Christianity was about a relationship with Jesus and the promise of eternal life. Looking back, I can see how inadequate this view of the Christian Gospel really was.

I can remember being taught about the Garden of Eden from my earliest childhood. I've got clear memories of the gripping story of Adam and Eve, of the apple and the snake. But I can't remember anyone explaining to me what it really meant!

No one explained to me that Adam and Eve's great sin of rebellion against God had created a wall of separation between God and me. No one taught me that if Adam had kept his part of the Covenant promise, the world would have been a very different place. No one helped me understand that if Adam had kept his promise then rebellion, sin, suffering and death would have been kept outside the perfection of the created order.

I was a follower of Jesus for several years before I came to understand the Fall, or to accept that it was because Adam broke his covenant with God that the world changed for the worse. I was well beyond my initial steps of discipleship before I grasped these fundamental truths about salvation.

I didn't understand that I was part of a fallen world of selfishness. A world in which God's laws had been rejected, disobeyed and dishonoured. A runaway world rushing headlong towards destruction. A broken world in which all the delicate harmonies of nature had been put out of tune and the innocence of humanity stripped away. A world under condemnation and under the judgement of God.

William Barclay records in his *Letters to the Galatians and Ephesians* that when Oscar Wilde tried to portray his own inner chaos he described the effect of this fallenness on each individual:

> The gods had given me almost everything. But I let myself be lured into long spells of senseless and sensual ease. Tired of being on the heights, I deliberately went to the depths in search of new sensation. What the paradox was to me in the sphere of thought, perversity became to me in the sphere of passion. I grew careless of the lives of others. I took pleasure where it pleased me, and passed on. I forgot that every little action of the common day

makes or unmakes character, and that therefore what one has done in the secret chamber, one has some day to cry aloud from the house-top. I ceased to be lord over myself. I was no longer the captain of my soul, and did not know it. I allowed pleasure to dominate me. I ended in horrible disgrace.

Several years ago, when I dramatized John Bunyan's *Pilgrim's Progress* for the stage show *Dangerous Journey*, I tried to make the 'slough of despond' as realistic as possible. Using a long run of ten-foot-high polythene sheeting, lurid red backlighting and stage smoke, we managed to create a dreadful spectacle. Beyond the polythene you could see the lost souls struggling to find some solid ground in a quicksand of despair. I loved the theatrical image we created because it portrayed what I'd eventually come to see as the 'fallenness' of all things.

I was several years down the track as a Christian before I really understood what it meant to be saved from the utter destruction all around me. Because I did not grasp the Fall, I did not grasp just how great was the mess that Jesus was pulling me out of. This lack of basic Christian teaching meant that my early growth as a Christian was really stunted.

The desperate state in which we live in this fallen world is summed up in a powerful prayer by William of St Thierry, who wrote

> How foolish we are to think that we can rule our own lives, satisfying our own desires, without thought of you. How stupid we are to imagine that we can keep our sins hidden. But although we may deceive other people, we cannot deceive you. And since you see into our hearts, we cannot deceive ourselves, for your light reveals to us our own spiritual corruption.

In my early years as a Christian, people didn't talk of sin, the Fall and impending judgement. It was all kept away from me. No one explained the desperate lostness of my state, and because I didn't understand, I didn't recognize what Jesus had actually done for me on the cross.

Hell

No one told me about hell. I came through a kind of Christian education in which, as far as I can remember, it was never mentioned. I'm sure this lack of teaching was a reaction to all those melodramatic Victorian lithographs of lakes of fire and tortured souls.

Looking back, however, I can see my Christian education lacked something crucial. I'm not suggesting that I should have been 'dangled over the pit' as a young child. Far from it. But someone should have told me about the reality of judgement and the existence of hell.

William Booth once apologized to a graduation class of young Salvation Army officers. He had kept them two years to teach them how to lead a person to Christ. It would be better, he said, had they spent five minutes in hell, because that way they could become really effective soul-winners. Maybe I, too, would have been a better Christian if I'd spent five minutes in hell. I now do believe in hell. I struggle to accept the fire and brimstone imagery of years gone by, but I know it as a spiritual certainty.

It's been my privilege over recent years to know the great preacher R.T. Kendall. His warmth as a friend and his hilarious sense of humour have been a constant encouragement to me, particularly in our travels in Israel together. We share a sense of awe about the things of God that is something akin to fear. In his book *Out of the Comfort Zone* Kendall wrote

> The teaching of Jesus regarding hell was not meant to make us comfortable. He had more to say about hell than he did about heaven. People sometimes say, 'I believe in heaven but I don't believe in hell.' I answer: if there is no hell, there is no heaven. The two rise or fall together. As for Jesus' teaching on hell, it blasts us out of our comfort zone. For the God who conceived of the teaching of hell and who created hell is not very nice. It's not my idea, I can assure you. No human being would have thought this up. But what if it is true?

I was never taught about hell, and because that piece of my early understanding was missing, I didn't fully recognize the importance of 'being saved', nor did I know the overwhelming joy of knowing that my destiny had been changed for eternity. I was denied a crucial part of the truth of Christian faith and experience.

I'm sure that some of my greatest heroes in the ministry have believed in hell, preached about it and been driven by an urgency and compassion to rescue people from it. Charles Wesley, for example, was a regular prison visitor at Newgate jail in London. He recorded in his journal that, while visiting a prisoner who was sick with fever and condemned to be hanged, he had explained to him the good news of the cross:

> I told him of one who came down from heaven to save lost sinners, and him in particular. I described the sufferings of the Son of God, his sufferings, agony and death. He listened with all the signs of eager astonishment; the tears trickled down his cheeks while he cried 'What? Was it for me? Did God suffer all this for so poor a creature as me?'

On the morning of the hanging, Charles went to meet the 'death cart' as it drove towards the gallows. There was a large crowd there, and they were taunting the prisoners. When the prisoner saw Charles, the guest preacher noticed that 'he smiled with the most composed, delightful countenance I ever saw.'

Charles mounted the death cart, and he and all the prisoners sang together

> Behold the Saviour of mankind
> Nailed to the shameful tree!
> How vast the love that him inclined
> To bleed and die for thee!
>
> 'Tis done! The precious ransom's paid;
> 'Receive My Soul,' he cries;
> See where he bows his sacred head!
> He bows his head, and dies!
>
> A guilty, weak and helpless worm,
> Into Thy hands I fall;
> Be Thou my life, my righteousness,
> My Jesus and my all.

'When the cart drew off,' wrote Charles, 'not one struggled for life. We left them going to meet their Lord.' Charles Wesley knew what it was to rescue people from the very pit of hell and to set their feet on the road to heaven.

I have known the reality of hell a number of times in my life. I've known it pastorally in sharing awful situations with people, and in glimpsing that sense of utter desolation which some of them have passed through. I've known it in my own life, in moments when I've let go of Christ and tried to live outside his grace or attempted to run away from his presence. I've known what the poet John Milton meant when he said, 'The mind is its own place, and in itself can make a heaven of hell, a hell of heaven.'

I'm sure that I have known a foretaste of hell on earth just as much as I have known a foretaste of heaven. Hell is a spiritual reality to me: it's that spiritual torment I've discovered when I've tried to live apart from the sustaining love of God. Sadly, for some this sense of desolation lasts for all eternity.

The power of the cross

I struggled into the lift at Gatwick airport. I was late for a plane and I was weighed down with three large cases. The lift was full, and I was the person nearest to the control panel. The lift only went up one level, so I pressed the button marked '1'. The door closed. Nothing happened. I pressed '1' again, and nothing happened. I pressed '0' and nothing happened. Eventually, goaded by a host of muttering passengers beside me, I opened the emergency panel and lifted the phone. After I'd explained our predicament to the emergency operator we waited for some considerable time.

Then, suddenly and unexpectedly, a man on the outside of the lift placed his fingers into the gap between the doors and pushed them open. We were astounded: we were still on the ground floor. We hadn't moved. And when the man said, 'Can I come in?' he was met with the chorus, 'But we want to get out!' It took a strong man on the outside to let us out.

I now see that my early years as a Christian were all the poorer because I didn't fully comprehend that Jesus had come to set me free. I didn't realize just how broken the world was, or why living for Jesus in such a fallen world could be so difficult. I would have looked at the world differently if I'd comprehended the Fall. I'd have loved Jesus more if I'd understood that he came not just to call me to follow him but to rescue me from a kind of entrapment to sin and personal rebellion against my Creator.

Now I know that God sent his only Son to put right what had gone wrong, and that he did it by shedding his blood on the cross. Now I understand that just as the first Adam was the source of death and judgement, this second 'Adam' came as the source of new life and salvation for me. The early church fathers saw the tree in the Garden of Eden which led to the Fall as a powerful image reflected in Calvary's tree at the end of Christ's life. Now I understand that when Jesus died on the tree on Calvary he transformed all that had resulted from Adam's disobedience at the first tree.

Now I know that the cross was the beginning of the end for the power of evil. Christ's saving work on the cross gives me the opportunity to know full forgiveness for all my sins and to enter into the promise that one day I will share in his ultimate victory.

My early years as a Christian disciple were very much focused on a relationship with Jesus, but it was some considerable time before I grasped what it meant to be 'saved'. My faith was more about a love-relationship with Jesus than about a mature trust that his death on the cross was the sole means of my forgiveness and salvation.

My experience of salvation crystallized for me one evening in the chapel at Cliff College. After a particularly poignant sermon about Jesus dying in my place on the cross, I was kneeling alone as the congregation was departing. One of my college peers, a student from Devon, whispered to me, 'Are you sure you're saved,

Rob? Because if you're not, why not make sure?' It was a very special moment for me. I certainly knew Jesus, and most definitely wanted to live my life for him. In that moment, however, on my knees in the college chapel, I confessed the sin and selfishness that were so prevalent in my life and claimed the forgiveness and cleansing of Jesus that were made available to me when he died on Calvary.

In that moment I recognized that I was a hopeless sinner and that only through Christ's death could I be forgiven and accepted. For me, as a Methodist, this personal experience was reminiscent of what had happened to John Wesley at a fellowship meeting in Aldersgate Street on 24 May 1738. He had already committed himself to a life of good works, had trained in theology and become an Anglican vicar, and he'd gone as a missionary to Georgia in the United States. He'd searched for authentic Christian faith. But that night he was able to say

> I felt my heart strangely warmed. I felt I did trust in Christ, Christ alone for my salvation; and an assurance was given me that he had taken away my sins, even mine, and saved me from the Law of sin and death.

As soon as the meeting in Aldersgate Street was over, John and several of his friends went to visit his brother Charles, who lived nearby. Charles Wesley's journal takes up the story:

> Towards ten, my brother was brought in triumph by a troop of our friends, and declared 'I believe!' We sang the hymn with great joy and parted with prayer.

John Wesley's experience became the hallmark of the early Methodist movement. On 29 November 1761 John Wesley wrote in his journal

Many have, and many do, daily experience an unspeakable change. After being deeply convinced of inbred sin, particularly of pride, anger, self-will and unbelief, in a moment they feel all faith and love; no pride, no self-will, or anger: and from that moment they have continual fellowship with God, always rejoicing, praying and giving thanks.

There has been a great deal of debate in the contemporary church about the message of the cross and what it really means today. I subscribe to the view that the cross has many layers of meaning, but I also believe that God's just anger with a rebellious and fallen world was assuaged by the death of his Son Jesus on the cross.

It was this message of 'saving grace' that Charles Wesley proclaimed to the prisoners in Newgate jail; it was a message that they found powerful and transformational. It was this message which enabled them to face the gallows with the assurance that they were truly accepted and forgiven. Why did no one tell me that Jesus came into the world to redeem it from its fallen state? That he came to save me from a world which had gone so tragically wrong? Could it be that those discipling me weren't sure if they believed it themselves? Could it be that they didn't accept that the brokenness of the world could only be put right by the One who had created it?

If I'd understood all this from the very beginning, a lot of other things would have made much more sense. I would have understood that a life lived for Jesus can't be easy in a world that has rejected God, a runaway world rushing headlong towards destruction.

In some Christian circles it still seems that it's very unpopular to teach new believers these fundamental truths about sin, faith and salvation. I've heard Christian leaders imply that 'if you've found Jesus, you've found the answer'. But the answer to what? If new believers don't comprehend the Fall, how can they possibly understand the purpose of Christ's coming or know the true joy of salvation from judgement?

Every new Christian deserves to be taught that Jesus came into a world populated by people who were bound by guilt, with no prospect of forgiveness, personal renewal or a new start. He came into a world which was bound by death, with no hope of eternal life or prospect of heaven. He came into a world bound by fear, where principalities and powers seemed to reign supreme. He came into a fallen world to set it free.

Over the years I've been exposed to many concepts and philosophies concerning the state of the world. Some seem to think that the world can be put right by some political agenda or through the teaching of some philosopher. The older I get as a Christian, however, the more stark is my view of the world. The longer I live, the more plain it seems to me that the world is in rebellion against God, and that the cause of its pain and trouble lies in this rejection of his love. It seems ever more clear to me that there is no way out in our own strength. We need the help of a Saviour who is greater than we are, and in whose love all the discordant notes of the universe can be brought back into harmony.

In four years of theological education I can't recall a single lecture on the theology of the cross or an introduction to the life-transforming effect which the death of Jesus can have. It's little wonder, then, that the lectures I received on pastoral care seemed so inadequate a preparation for some of the situations I have encountered in my ministry.

The address on the envelope read 'The Chapel', and as there was no letterbox in the church, the postman had pushed it under the front doors as best he could. The contents of the letter were bewildering. The writer, using prison notepaper, begged me to go to a nearby prison to visit him.

A week later, after all the formalities had been completed, I was led down a long grey corridor and into a small interview cell. Keys rattled, the lock turned, and I was led in to meet the prisoner. Two detectives arrived and sat behind me.

The prisoner had asked if he could make his confession to me, but with the police present. It was a horrific story of an axe murder and a life of sin. Eventually this man's life was transformed by the power of Christ. The prisoner could tell a new story: a story of repentance, forgiveness and a new beginning. I never cease to be amazed by the power of the Christian message of salvation. No matter how low we have sunk, how far we have strayed, or how foolish a life we have lived, there is room in the Calvary love of Jesus for forgiveness and a new beginning. Many of us who are long-established Christians need to discover again the transforming power of this redemption message.

Certainly my own pilgrimage to faith reached a point where I sensed that 'in my place condemned he stood' and believed that because the innocent Son of God died for me, my life could be transformed.

I wish someone had spelt this out for me sooner. I wish that someone in my preparation for ministry had taught me how to apply this message to real-life situations. I hope that the evangelists, pastors and preachers of the twenty-first century will be taught that the power for salvation does not lie in some spiritual 'feel good factor', but in the timeless message of the cross and in our desperate need for redemption and salvation.

The devil

The older I get, the more convinced I become that there is an active power of evil in the world. The old-fashioned images of a sooty-faced creature with horns don't seem credible to me: the devil is far more sophisticated than that. Yet no one in my early years of discipleship taught me about the devil, or made it clear to me how dangerous he could be to the development of my Christian life. In my early years as a Christian I had no understanding that I have authority over the evil one and so need never be afraid. No one explained that my old life was buried with Christ, and that I'd been raised to live a new life by his mighty power. I was now 'in Christ', and the power within me now was greater than the power that is in the world. If only I had been sent out into ministry with the words of Jesus to the returning seventy-two disciples ringing in my ears.

'I have given you authority to trample on snakes and scorpions and to overcome all the power of the enemy; nothing will harm you. However, do not rejoice that the spirits submit to you, but rejoice that your names are written in heaven' (Lk. 10:19-20).

Several years ago I was on a mission in Cyprus, and one afternoon I had the opportunity to go to the town of Paphos. The Roman governor Sergius Paulus used to live there many centuries ago. It was a great thrill to stand in the archaeological dig on the site of his palace and to see the beautiful mosaics in his reception hall. This was the very place where he would have interviewed Paul and Barnabas during their mission on the island. Paul's witness to the governor was a strategic part of his mission, but an evil magician called Bar-Jesus disrupted this work at every turn. Finally, Paul took authority over this man's evil ways and declared, 'You are a child of the devil and an enemy of everything that is right!' A thick mist came over the magician's eyes and, as a result, Sergius was won for Christ. If Paul had not confronted the works of the enemy, his mission would have been thwarted. Peter wrote

> Be self-controlled and alert. Your enemy the devil prowls around like a roaring lion, looking for someone to devour. Resist him, standing firm in the faith... (1 Pet. 5:8-9).

Sometimes in church life things seem to be falling apart. I've learnt to look behind the division, the discord and the lack of discipline to ask, 'Who's behind all this, and why?' Often, I've sensed that these are the works of the evil one being presented in human disguise. Paul wrote

> For our struggle is not against flesh and blood, but against the rulers, against the authorities, against the powers of this dark world and against the spiritual forces of evil in the heavenly realms (Eph. 6:12).

Spiritual warfare is an important everyday aspect of the life of prayer.

In the old pagan festival of Samhain, the forerunner of Hallowe'en, people lit bonfires to give light, threw nuts into them to make noise, disguised themselves with soot, and put evil-faced pumpkins around the village to ward off spirits. They did these things because they were afraid of the devil, and scared of what he might do to them. As Christians, however, we have no need to fear him, for as Paul wrote,

> ... having disarmed the powers and authorities, he made a public spectacle of them, triumphing over them by the cross (Col. 2:15).

We have the authority, in Christ, to dismiss the legions of the enemy.

I'm not one of those Christians who see demons around every comer or who live in a daily paranoia about the works of the evil one. I do believe, however, that Satan wants to confuse me and derail me, and that if I'm living my life in full surrender to Christ he will give me plenty of opposition.

Jesus saves me *now*

When I first became a Christian no one explained that I might fail God, that there would be times when I would sin, even as a Christian, and really mess up in my life as a disciple. There was an unspoken assumption among the older Christians who influenced me that once you'd found this 'salvation', life would be a bed of roses and that there would be nothing more to worry about. As time went by, however, I became more and more convinced that I could 'lose' this salvation.

When I was a student at Cliff College I used to do manual work in the college grounds a couple of times a week. The hours I spent in the garden were a good break from study, though I am no gardener. We used to talk and discuss as we worked – after all, a solid afternoon of weeding can be rather back-breaking!

One day I was working with a student whom I regarded as someone close to the Lord. We talked about our relationship with Christ, and I asked him about his faith. He told me that every week he spent an hour alone in the college chapel. He called it his weekly 'sorting out session' with the Lord. During that hour he would lay his life open before God and ask the Holy Spirit to pinpoint areas where he had failed. He told me that he would then confess his sins, claim forgiveness and ask the Lord to change him.

I've never forgotten that conversation, and ever since, I've seen confession as far more important than a 'sorry' prayer said before communion. The Lord's refining, purifying, recreating process should be continuing in our lives each week, and this demands time given over to honesty with God.

Each time I stop for a 'sorting out session' with the Lord, I find new areas of my life which need to be yielded to him. I need to learn how to rely more on him and less on myself. I need to receive the helpful and positive criticism of others. I want the lessons I learn from failure to become a growth point in my Christian life. I really do want him to correct the wrong attitudes which so affect me.

If I am to face up to the reality of my sin, I need to be really specific. It was the custom for people at Wesley's class meetings to confess their sins to each other and to encourage one another in the life of holiness. This was real confession – heartfelt, embarrassing, humbling. The Lord can really work with people who are willing to be honest with him.

I need to be specific in my prayers of confession. Sometimes I've even made a written list of sins and asked the Lord to deal with them one by one. It can be a painful experience, but one which is a vital aspect of my life of prayer.

Sadly, it took me many years before I learnt the benefits of mourning for my past sins, or found the gift of sombre introspection. Rather, I loaded my diary with hasty plans to fill my days. I scheduled myself into the emptiness of busy days. I made plans for what will be, preferring the excitement of a clean-sheet future to facing up to the harsh realities of yesterday. I am part of a generation that lives for what will be, but with little understanding of saying sorry for what has been.

I have measured myself against those of lesser stature; judged my performance against the mediocre reputations of my peers; congratulated myself on a job well done and commended myself for a life well lived. I've rewarded myself because I made the best of what I had.

There have been many times when I have needed to look back down the winding road of memory and discover that I still had much to learn. Times when I needed to retrace my steps down the track of personal experience and to see just how much I had failed him. I have needed to make a journey of honest introspection with Jesus as my Guide.

Thank goodness that my companion on this journey to my past is kind, for his grace has already covered a multitude of sins. My Saviour Guide would rather redeem my past than use it in evidence against me.

He is a friendly guide who doesn't come in judgement but with a love far deeper than I can ever understand. He invites me to gaze back down the road I've travelled and to see the rich panoply of experiences spread out across the plains of memory.

If I do not take this introspective journey I'll live a lie supported by the figments of my own imagination.

For me, reality is facing the truth of what I've failed to be; it's recognizing that even when I chose the higher cause my motives were mixed. Sadly, my ambitions were often driven by darker forces.

Reality is a journey backwards to look into the faces of the ones I've hurt. It's allowing him to point out the well-marked signs I missed along the way. It's understanding how things could have been if only I'd gone his way. Reality is what's written on the sad, hurting faces of those who I passed by on the other side. Reality is forgotten promises, selfish relationships, well-shaped lies. Reality is seeing how I've changed. It's recognising how the long years of self-seeking have tarnished me, how the face of my public image masked my true identity. Reality is grieving over the high ideals of youth, now levelled by the complex compromises of a busy life. It's understanding how my bright, trusting faith as a new believer grew shabby and dulled by a dirty world. Reality is seeing myself as I really am, not as I would like to be seen. Seeing myself as he sees me, with all his omniscient insight of the years and his understanding of who I truly am.

This, then, is where the mourning starts. My gentle Guide must bring me to the place of truth so that the pain of it might unplug the wellspring of my tears and drive me to my knees.

When Jesus cried, 'It is finished!' he said it all. He wasn't saying, 'I'm finished,' but rather, 'I've finished the work that I came to do.' The sacrifice was complete, and by dying on the cross he had won salvation for us. I receive this forgiveness as a free gift or I don't receive it at all. I can certainly never deserve it.

When I have a 'sorting out session' with the Lord, I aim for it to be honest, real and thorough. Unless I lay my life before him and allow the searchlight of his holiness to rest upon me, those wrong things in my life can never be dealt with. No one explained this when I first became a Christian. No one pointed out that although the work of salvation is complete the moment I trust in Jesus, it's a work that continues within me for the rest of my life.

The *Daybreak* musical tour was absolutely exhausting. Every day we travelled to a different town to set up several tons of equipment, rehearse the local choirs and drama groups, and present the musical to a packed theatre. I played the part of Simon Peter. Night after night I had to stand alone on the stage in a blinding spotlight and enact his denial.

As the last chords of the last song faded, the lengthy de-rig in Southampton Guildhall began. Props, costumes and PA equipment were packed and trundled on trolleys to the waiting truck.

I looked up at the Guildhall clock; it was just after midnight. It was my turn to travel overnight in the truck. I clambered into the cab next to the driver and wrapped my coat around me. We were bound for Cornwall: it was going to be a very long night.

The roads were covered with mist. The noise of the engine made conversation impossible; and no matter how I tried, I couldn't find a comfortable position for sleep.

Hour after hour we rolled along. My thoughts turned back to the previous evening's performance. The sounds and images rolled around my mind and I relived Peter's denial. I looked again at my own life, and Peter's words returned to haunt me. The swirling mist in front of the headlights created an eerie feeling of unreality.

As my mind backtracked down the years I began to feel a failure as a disciple of Jesus. I felt that there were areas of my life which I still needed to yield to his lordship. I felt that I loved the work more than I loved the Lord.

As soon as we arrived in Cornwall I found a room and knelt to pray. I was broken. I offered every aspect of my life and ministry back to the Lord and asked him to change me from within.

There have been many occasions when I have laid my life before the Lord and asked him to reveal those things which need to be changed within me. Many times when I've felt the need to be real with him, to be honest with him – and to come back to him.

Some words from the first letter of John have been an enormous strength to me throughout my life. They remind me of two things: first that honest confession is an integral part of Christian living, and secondly that Christ's forgiveness is ongoing. It reads

> If we claim to be without sin, we deceive ourselves and the truth is not in us. If we confess our sins, he is faithful and just and will forgive us our sins and purify us from all unrighteousness (1 Jn. 1:8-9).

No one told me, but now I see that his work of transformation and change within me is an ongoing process. Time and again I've had to return to the Lord and ask him to deal with aspects of my being which I know have displeased him. When I feel that I've failed, I have to face up to my sin and remember again the breadth of his redeeming power.

I have a friend who is the minister of a small Yorkshire chapel. He is a keen artist, and often involves the whole congregation in celebrating their faith creatively. One Sunday I watched as his congregation turned up with all kinds of rubbish they'd collected: scrap paper, empty boxes and useless trash. Gradually they sorted through the refuse, and over the days that followed they discovered ways of using it artistically.

By the following Sunday the mound of rubbish had been transformed into a powerful illustration of the cross. The twisted, broken scraps of refuse had been redeemed into something beautiful and elegant.

This is the ongoing work of redemption. This is what the Lord wants to do within us all, if only we'll let him. He wants to take away the filth and sin of our lives and forgive us. He wants to take away the guilt and shame and transform us. He wants to turn us away from selfishness and redirect us. A very old Gospel hymn, which I used to sing as a teenager, has become increasingly important to me over the years. The simple refrain is, 'Jesus saves me now, Jesus saves me all the time, Jesus saves me now.' Now I understand that although I received salvation in the moment that I trusted Christ, I still stand in need of his work of salvation every moment of every day. His salvation is ongoing, active, still transforming me. As I come back to him again and again, his work in me is gradually refining me and still changing me.

Canon Michael Green said, 'All other great teachers said, "Follow that," but he claimed to be the truth and said, "Follow me."'

Once I was Christmas shopping with my family in London's busy Oxford Street. I'm not that keen on shopping at the best of times, but among the jostling crowds in central London that day I was finding it more trying than usual. While my family went to buy some Christmas decorations I escaped for a few minutes of peace and quiet. I wandered into a rather exclusive department store and took the escalator down to a different world. It was good to be away from the crowds.

The china department was beautifully laid out, with spotlighted dinner services, shelves full of delicate china, and figurines on pedestals. I looked at a few of the price tags: everything was out of my range.

I ambled past one of the enormous display cases and found, to my amazement, a potter hunched over his wheel. In his stained overalls he looked quite out of place in such a sumptuous setting. He was engrossed in his work. A group of shop assistants meandered into the department; they were on their lunch break. For a while they stood and watched him, then one of the girls asked if she could have a try. He graciously stepped aside, and the girl moved over to the wheel and took the half-shaped clay.

She pressed the pedal, the wheel turned, and gradually the pot was formed. For some moments the crowd stood in amazement as the wet, grey clay rose uncertainly above the wheel.

Suddenly the shape collapsed, fell off the wheel and crumpled onto the floor beside her. Her clothes were splattered with clay and she looked annoyed. The group of shop girls laughed and sauntered away, their voices fading as they left the department.

I was just about to leave too, when I noticed the potter looking down at the lump of clay on the floor. He bent down and patiently placed it back on the wheel. He set the wheel spinning, and in his eyes I could see the vision of what it would become.

His fingers moved deftly over the spinning mass; moulding, guiding, forming. The clay slowly took shape. At last the wheel stopped. He had made a perfect vase. He gently removed it from the wheel and placed it on the workbench beside him. It was complete.

The Lord told the prophet Jeremiah to go and watch a potter at work. As he watched, the potter took a misshapen piece of clay and began to rework it. The potter took something ruined and formed perfection from it. And the Lord said, 'O house of Israel, can I not do with you as this potter does?' (Jer. 18:6).

This Creator God who set the stars in place and who coloured the rainbow's arch wants to shape my life. This God, who made the world such a beautiful place, wants to make me a beautiful person too. I can't make anything out of myself that has the right shape or purpose unless I place my life in his hands. I may struggle and strain, I may exhaust myself in the heat of my effort, but I will only create a disfigured life. When I was a student I lay on the floor of my college room in absolute brokenness. I recognized that I was utterly and completely dependent on Christ, and him alone. I confessed that I was nothing and, in brokenness, cast myself upon his love. I felt that I was offering myself like clay in the Potter's hand, and allowing him to shape my life as it should really be.

Anyone who has been to the amazing museum of D-Day at Caen can't fail to have been impressed by the big-screen portrayal of the events in that invasion. On one screen you see the assault from the perspective of the Allied forces, from cameras on ships and in landing craft, as the troops make for the beaches and engage in heavy fighting. Beside it, on the other, you see the invasion from cameras installed in bunkers and gun emplacements on the Nazi side.

After initial heavy fighting, the Allied troops gain a foothold and gradually press forward, taking territory, until at last they have supremacy. Then they commit forces to mopping up resistance and finishing the job. In some sense I see in this a reflection of the battle in my own story. Once Jesus had made a bridgehead into my life, he had taken ultimate control, but there

were still 'pockets of resistance' within me which he
continued to tackle. The work of salvation continues in
me, with my agreement and utter surrender to God, to
this day. His work in me will not be finished this side
of eternity. I don't think anyone ever explained this to
me in the early years of my discipleship, and it would
have been most helpful if they had.

True believing

Throughout my ministry I have been known as an
evangelical Christian. This has certainly been a mixed
blessing. It has meant that in many ecclesiastical
settings I have been pigeon-holed, and my contribution
to serious debate has sometimes been discounted.

There were some particularly tough times at
theological college, when to be considered evangelical
was to be marginalized and sometimes even mocked.
In the church denomination in which I was reared it
has certainly not been very popular to take this
standpoint. Over the years I have tried to nurture,
encourage and support a number of younger evangelical
ministers who have felt marginalized and hurt because
they were not taken seriously. Some carried the label
'fundamentalist' and were even considered disreputable
as a result.

In a society where other religions are becoming
increasingly militant and strident, an 'anything goes'
Christian theology must become increasingly irrelevant
and powerless.

The time has come for Christians to rediscover the
core elements of their believing, to learn how to defend
them and to live in their spiritual reality. If the church
does not facilitate the rising generation of young leaders

to do this, we will let them loose into an ever darker world without the spiritual wherewithal to cope.

I did not become an evangelical Christian because I was mentored or discipled in that way. I have arrived at this theological position through a lifetime of study, reading, debate and pastoral experience.

Looking back to some of the young leaders who were my peers and who despised my theological position, it's disturbing to see how few remain in the Christian ministry, and how many ministries have been shipwrecked by the storms of life along the way.

A lot of what I was taught at theological college was destructive to faith and detrimental to the development of a mature spirituality. I was subjected to a sneering intellectualism which despised any sense that the Bible is true, and which often twisted the historic creeds of the church to create new meanings which were far from biblical.

Dietrich Bonhoeffer wrote

> Cheap grace means justification of sin but not of the sinner … It is preaching forgiveness without repentance; it is baptism without the discipline of community; it is the Lord's Supper without confession of sin; it is absolution without personal confession. Cheap grace is grace without discipleship, grace without the cross, grace without the living, incarnate Jesus Christ.

I wish someone had warned me when I first became a Christian that some Christian leaders do not uphold the faith. There are some preachers who do not proclaim the historic creeds. There are some Bible scholars who seem more intent on destroying God's Word than on expounding it. One of the favourite Bible scholars of some of my theological tutors was Rudolf Bultmann, the German New Testament scholar, who wrote

> It is impossible to use electric light and the wireless and to avail ourselves of modern medical and surgical discoveries, and at the same time to believe in the New Testament world of spirits and miracles.

In an age of web and cyberspace, of Mars missions and genetics, however, I still find it easy to believe in the New Testament world of spirits and miracles.

Some Christian leaders seem to be immersed in a kind of Christian believing which Richard Niebuhr once described in this way:

> A God without wrath brought men without sin into a kingdom without judgement through the ministrations of a Christ without a cross.

Many ordinary people see the church as inept, powerless, irrelevant, compromised and with nothing to say. Opinion polls and market research indicate that they are turned off by statements from Christian leaders. Perhaps our credibility is undermined because many ordinary people perceive that we don't really believe. Peter wrote

> We did not follow cleverly invented stories when we told you about the power and coming of our Lord Jesus Christ, but we were eye-witnesses of his majesty. ... We ourselves heard this voice that came from heaven when we were with him on the sacred mountain (2 Pet. 1:16,18).

Historian Sir James Frazer said that 'the doubts which have been cast on the historical reality of Jesus are, in my judgement, unworthy of serious attention'.

J.N. Geldenhuys explained that 'the whole course of world history during the last nineteen hundred years is inexplicable apart from the historical fact that Jesus Christ lived, died and rose again'.

William Lecky noted that 'the simple record of these three short years of active life has done more to regenerate and soften mankind than all the disquisitions of philosophers and the exhortations of moralists'. James Irwin, the astronaut who walked on the moon, said, 'It is more significant that God walked on earth than that man walked on the moon.'

Yet many of our national Christian leaders are known by their public statements of disbelief and their questioning of the historic creeds. Could it be that the church is reaping what it has sown? If we do not really believe in a fallen world, if we don't fear judgement and hell, if we don't warn of a Destroyer who can tear us apart or proclaim a Saviour who can rescue us and prepare us for heaven, then what shall we speak of? The Christian church has nothing to say if it does not speak from its biblical foundation and does not engage with the spiritual realities which make it the world's greatest faith community. No one warned me of the danger of false believing.

2

What they didn't tell me about discipleship

Commitment

Herbert Silverwood, the Cliff College evangelist and open-air preacher, came to encourage me when I was leading one of my first missions. I was just twenty-one years of age, and he was well into his eighties. He came and slept on the floor in a church vestry, and refused the coach fare I offered him. He travelled hundreds of miles just to support me. His encouragement in those early days was very important to me. In those days he drew great crowds whenever he preached in the open air. He told wonderful stories and great jokes and subtly applied them to the Christian life. His last instruction to me was that I should 'lift Jesus high so that many may be drawn to him'.

Whenever Herbert made an appeal, his voice trembled with emotion and he would talk of how he first heard the Gospel as a 'cursin and swearin' Yorkshire pit lad, and how, when he responded, he felt different to anything he'd ever felt before.

Herbert challenged me to make open appeals on every possible occasion and to call people to salvation whenever I could. His challenge has affected my whole ministry, and ever since, calling people to receive salvation has been a central part of my ministry. Even now, some thirty years later, I make an open appeal at the end of nearly every sermon. Some people don't like it, saying that they find it off-putting or overly emotional, but I make no apologies for doing it. In my opinion, far too few preachers ever make this kind of invitation, so I consider it my responsibility to do what I can to get the message out.

An open appeal puts people on the spot, presents a choice, and makes a life-changing challenge. It's been an integral part of the mission hall tradition in which I was reared, and my own response to appeals such as this has played a special part in my discipleship. I believe it's also been important for many others. When I make an appeal I always try to respond to it first. As I invite others to come forward, I want them to join me because I, too, am a 'sinner at the foot of the cross' who stands alongside them in the need of prayer. When I make my personal response in this way it's not a performance but a genuine offering of myself to Christ again.

It's just as well that I regularly find myself at the foot of the cross again. Just when I think I'm 'doing well' as a follower of Jesus, something always reminds me that I'm not OK, and that I need to come back to the beginning and offer my life again.

I wish someone had explained what Christian commitment really entails, for it took me many years to come to terms with it. No one ever explained to me that Christian commitment was not a one-off response, but something which would be ongoing throughout the rest of my life. True commitment is about continuing to yield every day. It's an ongoing surrender and it's an integral aspect of true discipleship. It needs to be worked out in a myriad ways in our everyday life.

Cost

When I take pilgrims to the Holy Land, I insist that the tour guide gives us plenty of time at the Garden of Gethsemane. It has a powerful effect on the group, and although I have been there several times, it still has a powerful effect on me.

After we've walked the steep path down the Mount of Olives, we reach the postcard and trinket sellers and enter a quiet garden which is still shaded by an ancient olive grove. Beyond the garden is a beautiful church, and when we go inside, its purple windows create a dark and moody atmosphere. This church captures the intensity of Jesus' Gethsemane struggle. At the centre of the sanctuary is a large outcrop of rock surrounded by a little fence. The last time I visited the church, an elderly nun opened a gate and beckoned me through. I sank to my knees and rested my forehead on the rough rock. I don't know if this was the rock where Jesus agonized over God's call on his life, but it was a solemn reminder of his personal anguish on Passover night.

In Gethsemane, Jesus was struggling with his Father's will. It was an intense struggle, because he knew that the days ahead would involve awful suffering and rejection. Was he really prepared to walk the lonely road of suffering to the cross? His inner anguish culminated in the words, 'Take this cup away from me; yet not my will, but yours be done' (Lk. 22:42).

I never grasped the intensity of his surrender until I knelt there at the Gethsemane rock. I began to understand the dreadful reality of what faced him, and glimpsed the true cost of his obedience.

This was a gut-wrenching, life-threatening, all-or-nothing kind of commitment. This Gethsemane prayer was a desperate cry from the heart in the midst of the supernatural struggle between the forces of good and evil. The devil's agenda was about Jesus taking the easy road, avoiding the cross and saving his own life. The Father, however, saw the suffering and crucifixion that awaited his Son, and the obedience which would result in salvation for the world.

Gethsemane was a spiritual struggle between the forces of good and evil. It was reminiscent of the forty days which Jesus spent in the wilderness on the Mount of Temptation. It was a battle which had to be fought mentally, emotionally and spiritually. It was a battle so intense that beads of sweat poured down his face and fell to the ground like drops of blood. It was a struggle which some scholars believe was so stressful that it could have killed him.

In that dark Gethsemane garden Jesus surrendered himself to the will of God. In doing so, he made an act of supreme personal sacrifice. This wasn't a sentimental kind of commitment, for it demanded everything. This was no 'shed a tear, say a prayer and move on' kind of response. It was the costly template for all genuine Christian commitment.

No one helped me to grasp what that really meant in my life. In my early life as a Christian I saw commitment in raw emotional terms. It was about 'going forward' in public response; about singing 'Take my life and let it be'; about heartfelt prayers of submission. It was something you said rather than something that you worked out in the way you lived. Now I know that an emotional response is only the starting gate for Christian commitment. 'Surrender to Christ' is not a once-and-for-all experience reserved for special missions or events. It's something which must be woven into the texture of daily life.

Some Christians seem to handle this kind of commitment with ease. They never admit to struggling with the cost of it. I wish that I were so fortunate. To be honest, I empathize with Jesus in his struggle in Gethsemane. In my life, Christian commitment has sometimes been almost too much to bear. True commitment means doing things we don't want to do, going to places where we don't want to go and relating to people we'd prefer never to meet. It's worked out in painful decisions and made real in the big personal battles which we face.

No one explained to me just how tough it would be to translate Christian commitment into the complexities of everyday life. No one warned me how hard it would be to work out what it really means in a world where things aren't black and white. A lifestyle of Christian commitment involves real sacrifices.

I live in a very 'me-focused' society. My natural inclination is to prioritize around 'my' needs, 'my' living standards and 'my' aspirations. When I start to live with a God-centred set of priorities, however, I discover that I've begun to embark on a counter-cultural way of life. Tom Sine, the American writer and preacher, has spent much of his ministry questioning the comfortable lifestyle of middle America. He has made himself quite unpopular in some quarters as a result. Listening to his teaching can be an uncomfortable experience. When I had breakfast with him recently, however, I found him to be very warm and amicable. In *Living on Purpose* Sine reminds us ...

> The call to follow Christ was an invitation to a whole life faith that was profoundly counter-cultural, both then and now. Those first disciples never settled for the kind of narrow, disengaged faith that has become normative

today. They understood that following Jesus was a whole life proposition.

Tom Sine is right. Many of us have made a Christian commitment which we haven't translated into the reality of everyday life.

Over the last few years it's been my privilege to get to know some of the Christian politicians in the major parties. For some of them, the cost of discipleship has been very real.

Sir Brian Mawhinney has been a great encouragement to the various Christian fellowship groups in Parliament over many years. In the last couple of years I've been grateful for his advice regarding the defence of religious freedoms in the UK. He served in John Major's cabinet and has been portrayed as a tough and ruthless politician.

There were times in his political career when Sir Brian's determination to uphold Christian standards brought strong criticism and condemnation. Once he ordered that some explicit sex education material be destroyed because the relevant authorities had not been properly consulted. It was a decision which brought derision from sections of the national press. In his book *In the Firing Line* he discussed which of the Ten Commandments he found the hardest to follow, and concluded that it was the first.

> It establishes the pre-eminence of God and the paramount need for man to worship. Breaking it – living without Jesus – means putting something or someone else at the centre of our lives. Whatever that is, it becomes our 'god' and our daily motivation. Like many others, I find that the First Commandment is the sternest test of my life and thinking. Breaking it, by substituting another 'god', undermines tranquillity and destroys contentment.

Sir Brian is right: Christian commitment is about a rigorous kind of self-examination which asks 'who' or 'what' is my God? It's echoed in Rick Warren's challenging book *The Purpose-Driven Life*:

> What will be the centre of my life? This is the question of worship. Who are you going to live for? You can centre your life around your career, family, sport or hobby. You can live for money, having fun, or many other activities. These are all good things, but they don't belong at the centre of your life. None is strong enough to hold you together when life starts breaking apart. You need an unshakeable centre. Actually, whatever is at the centre of your life is your god.

The centrality of Jesus in our lives should mean that he shapes everything. He becomes the manager of our priorities, the master of our finances, the controller of our time, the director of our emotions and the Lord of our destiny. True commitment needs to be unpacked in a thousand small decisions every day. It's about how we actually live rather than how we intend to live; it's about saying 'no' to the world and 'yes' to God. It's about reordering our priorities and about serving the needs of others more than our own. It took me too long to recognize that commitment without action leads to a stunted kind of Christianity. True Christian commitment is about making a real difference in the world. Without it, Christianity is nothing more than a comforting blanket of self-centred emotion.

Obedience

I was taught that God guides, that he has a plan for us and that he always makes his way plain. When I became a Christian I believed that I was handing over the future direction of my life and putting it under Christ's authority. No one explained just how difficult it would be to discover his will, however, or what I had to do if I misread it, took a wrong turn or made a wrong decision. No one warned me that sometimes his perfect plan could be thwarted by the disobedience of others.

I believed that to be yoked to Christ meant what it implied: I would be blinkered while he steered. In the early years of my Christian life I tried to live according to his invitation:

> 'Take my yoke upon you and learn from me, for I am gentle and humble in heart, and you will find rest for your souls. For my yoke is easy and my burden is light' (Mt. 11:29-30).

Once I visited the tiny island of Sark, which is a short boat ride from Guernsey. No cars are permitted on the island, but near the jetty where the ferry pulls in there is a taxi-rank of horses and carts. Most of the 'round the island tours' were beyond my price range, but at the very end of the line was an elderly driver with an equally elderly horse, and he was willing to do a deal. Beaming at me with his one tooth, he explained that he'd only ever left Sark once – on a day trip to Guernsey. He hadn't enjoyed the experience.

The family and I climbed aboard the rickety old cart for a grand tour of the island. The horse clip-clopped ahead of us and the cart rattled and shook as we drove along the dusty track. As the tour progressed, the driver handed the reins over to my young son. I was worried. The boy hardly knew right from left, and as we drove past the clifftops I wondered if we might roll over.

When my son pulled right we turned right, and when he pulled left we turned left. The blinkered horse had no idea where he was heading; he simply obeyed. He trusted the driver implicitly.

As I have sought to know Christ's guidance for my life, I have often remembered the blind obedience of that old workhorse. I have tried to 'wear the yoke' and to trust his tug of the rein. I've believed this to be an integral part of what it is to be his disciple.

I wish that someone had warned me, however, that there would be days in my Christian life when I would be very confused about which way the rein was being tugged, or which path he wanted me to follow.

I have known occasions when I genuinely didn't know what to do for the best, times when there seemed no tug on the reins at all. Times when I longed for the Lord just to part the sky and point me in one direction or another. Times when I wanted to hear him say, 'This is the way; walk in it' (Is. 30:21). No one told me what to do when I was as confused as this. I've heard some remarkable testimonies to God's immediate and specific guidance in the lives of others, but it rarely worked out like that for me.

Late one night I was driving through France in a heavy thunderstorm. I was tired, disorientated and completely lost. Through the blur created by the windscreen wipers I could see a T-junction, and I had two choices – to turn left or right.

Then my headlights picked out a road sign which offered two alternatives. 'Toutes directions' and 'Toutes autres directions'. The choice of 'all directions' and 'all other directions' was the most unhelpful possible! God's plan has sometimes seemed just as obscure, and I've sometimes felt very confused about the way ahead. I've met many Christians who have come to similar unsigned crossroads in their lives: 'this job or that', 'this college or that', 'this relationship or that,' 'this career move or that,' and even 'this church or that'. I was taught that God guides us through Scripture, but I've sometimes sat with my Bible open looking for 'a word' that would show me which way to go, yet found that nothing came.

I was taught that God guides us through the wisdom of other Christians, but sometimes when I've asked for this kind of advice, I've been told, 'I haven't a clue'.

I was taught that God guides us through the Holy Spirit, and that I would know instinctively which way I should go. But I have sometimes sat bewildered. One minute I felt that God was saying one thing and the next something completely different.

These foggy experiences have been very disturbing. Why didn't God make his will more plain? Was it him or me who was to blame? I'm very sceptical of books which bring guidance down to 'ten easy steps to discern God's will'. To me, it's often seemed more like a thousand steps, and even when I've followed them I wasn't sure if I was on the right track. No one warned me that seeking God's will could be this confusing.

I've sought God's guidance in many situations, and I've been desperate to know his will. There were times when I asked: should I become minister of this church, or that? Accept the invitation to do this piece of work, or that? Employ this member of staff, or that? Write this book, or that? Move this way, or that? Send the kids to this school, or that? Devote my time to this good cause, or that?

Sometimes I've tried to rid myself of human bias and to lay it all before God, saying, 'I don't mind which way, just *tell* me!' But the silence has been deafening. No one told me that guidance could be such a maze.

At times like this I go back to the story in Acts 16:6-8, describing what happened to Paul:

> Paul and his companions travelled throughout the region of Phrygia and Galatia, having been kept by the Holy Spirit from preaching the word in the province of Asia. When they came to the border of Mysia, they tried to enter Bithynia, but the Spirit of Jesus would not allow them to. So they passed by Mysia and went down to Troas.

These verses tell of what must have been a very stressful time in Paul's ministry. He wanted to preach in Asia and Bithynia (and probably in Mysia too). I'm sure that when he set out he prayed about his mission and felt that he was following God's leading.

Paul knew that reaching the people of this region was important to God. Having determined what God wanted, he set out on the journey. But while he was in transit the plan was constantly changing.

This insight has really helped me. Paul didn't sit around waiting for 'sealed orders' for years on end. He surrendered to Christ, determined what God wanted, and got going.

On the journey, he was prevented from going where he thought he had been sent, so he looked for a new plan even while he was travelling. I wonder what was really happening in this situation, and smile at the possibilities. When Paul was kept by the Holy Spirit from preaching the Word of God in the province of Asia, what was the real reason? Did he run out of money, miss the camel train, overshoot the turning, meet someone who told him that Asian food wouldn't suit him, get a hunch that the natives weren't friendly or meet a Roman soldier who said there'd be trouble if he went that way?

When he reached the road to Bithynia and the Spirit of Jesus wouldn't let him take it, what was really going on? Did he have an overwhelming sense of dread, a spiritual hunch, or some prophetic insight? Whichever it was, Paul knew he couldn't go where he thought he was called to go. In my time I've adopted a very pragmatic style when it comes to determining God's will. I see his will as something alive, interactive and real. It unfolds with the events of my life and is shaped by the ever-changing circumstances of my life.

I am writing this chapter in the United States, where everyone seems to have digital voice guidance systems in their car. The gravel-voiced automaton guides you step by step along your journey. It only needs two pieces of information: where you are and where you want to go. It never starts its instructions with the words, 'If I was going there, I wouldn't start from here.' God's guidance begins where we are, rather than where we were supposed to be. When God guided Jonah in the belly of the big fish, he didn't start with the words, 'You were supposed to be on a boat to Nineveh.' No, God started where Jonah was, and took him back to the place where he was originally supposed to be.

I can only know God's will when I am wholeheartedly committed to him and surrendered to his purposes. When that's in place I can confidently set off on the journey and trust that he knows the way.

Sometimes Christians stick religiously to their 'ten easy steps' philosophy of guidance but remain stuck at the starting gate, waiting for years until they receive 'a word from God'. Precious time is wasted when all God really wanted them to do was to set off, and to follow Paul's example in Acts by following their nose until the Lord 'put it out of joint'!

Paul set out with a heart surrendered and a vision to fulfil. He tried every door along the way, and persisted on the journey until he could go no further. When he reached Troas he was at the end of the road, with only the sea ahead. Only then, when he could go no further, did God reveal the man from Macedonia and let Paul hear the words 'Come over and help us.' I've discovered this evolutionary nature of God's guidance time and again. If I set out with a heart surrendered and a 'mission to fulfil', he guides me in the many decisions which shape the direction of my journey.

I love ships. It doesn't matter if they're ocean-going liners or simple rowing boats. For me, there's nothing better than messing around in boats. It's been my privilege to steer boats of many kinds. I've taken the helm of three-masted yachts, the wheel of speedboats, and the tiller of canal barges. Whatever the vessel, however, it's always much easier to steer it when it's under way than when it's stationary. A boat becalmed or with engine failure, or whose oarsman is taking a rest, is practically impossible to steer. But get some speed up and the slightest tilt of the tiller or stroke of the oar can make a huge impact on the course ahead. No one told me when I became a Christian that God doesn't guide in 'ten easy steps'. No one explained that his guidance is interactive, alive and ongoing. No one showed me that he can guide us while we're in motion and can change our course while we're actually 'under way'.

What God looks for is a heart surrendered and a will yielded to him. He doesn't expect the rest of life to be put on hold until we know the way. I'm sure there have been occasions when I've interpreted his will in the wrong way. Times when, while my heart was surrendered to him, my logic, my prejudice, my emotions or my gut instincts got in the way and sent me hurtling down the wrong path. No one warned me that I could misread his guidance, or make wrong choices which could have far-reaching implications for my life and the lives of others.

I've met Christians who have been frozen into inaction when they felt they got things wrong and misread his will. Just a few days ago I met a lawyer who had left a successful career to follow a vocation in Christian service. It had all gone wrong, however, and he was trying to re-enter the profession he had so recently left. He had been devastated by the experience and was asking me, 'Where is God's guidance in this?'

Many sincere Christians have lost confidence in their ability to hear him, and live in fear that they might get it wrong again. Some, like the lawyer I met, live under a cloud of what could have been or what should not have been. This isn't healthy or helpful.

One of my heroes is George Verwer, the founder of Operation Mobilisation, one of the most effective mission agencies of my generation. It's a movement which has mobilized tens of thousands of young people into a ministry of evangelism. George has cropped up again and again in my life just when I seemed to need a bit of encouragement or a new challenge to serve God in mission. One of the sayings which I have often heard him repeat has really encouraged me. He says, 'I believe that God has plans A to Z for our lives. "A" is his best, and "Z" the worst. I've messed up so often that I think I'm on plan T, but he's still got a plan, and I still want to follow it.'

If George Verwer is on plan T and God is still using him so effectively, there is hope for the rest of us! I sometimes think that I'm on plan Z, but even here he still has a direction for my life and a plan for me to fulfil. It's been my privilege to share this insight with others, and to see their eyes light up with new hope. The young Christian girl, unmarried yet pregnant, whose vocation lies in ruins. The young Christian prisoner, his life in shreds and his career plan now unusable. The young Christian student, clutching a letter from the university Dean to say he's messed up his exams and can't resit. The young minister, facing a moral charge that will disbar him from continuing in ministry. There are so many people who through some personal failure have missed God's plan 'A' for their lives: So many people who need to discover that God still has a purpose and a future for them.

God's will doesn't come in a plain brown envelope as sealed orders at the start of our Christian journey. Those who intimate that it does, or that we can know it through 'ten easy steps', are sadly misguided. No, God's will is alive, it's messy and forever responsive to the changing circumstances of real life, real people and real situations.

God's guidance is not a career plan set in stone. It's shaped by where we've been. He meets us where we are and relates to the choices we face today. Even when we have failed, he picks us up and sends us on a different but nonetheless deeply enriching journey. Sometimes, that journey ends up on the road which we were originally intended to travel.

If we are to fulfil his purposes we need a heart surrendered and a heartfelt desire to become the people he wants us to be. He's not looking for servants who will spend their life hanging around and waiting, he's looking for those who have a vision to fulfil and a passion to see it come on earth. No one told me that God's guidance swings into action when we just 'get going'.

Rejection

When I became a Christian I learnt about persecution and the supreme sacrifice that some are called to make in the service of Christ. No one explained to me that there is still a cost to Christian commitment even when you live in a 'Christian' country and in a relatively supportive context. It is, of course, a much more insipid kind of opposition than that faced by those who end up tortured or in prison, but it can still involve painful experiences of rejection if we are unwavering in our Christian commitment. If we are really living for God, we may well be targeted by those who think we are stupid or infantile. Our surrender to Christ can lead to others making us feel inferior and cutting us out of the 'in' group.

I once presented a radio programme which contained interviews with Christians in the Royal Navy. One young rating had made a nice income on the side by distributing porn magazines to his ship's company. On one home leave he was dramatically converted to Christ and returned to his ship a very different man.

He gave up his 'porn paper round', and it was taken over by another rating. The second rating told me, 'I took over the distribution of porn, and sold it just as he had. I made it my personal mission to humiliate him on every occasion I could. I was sure I could persuade him to turn back to his old ways and to distribute the porn again. But the reverse happened. And eventually he led me to Christ.'

The humiliation suffered by that first rating must have been tough, but he displayed a grace and forgiveness which had such a powerful influence on the one who taunted him that it changed his life. His new Christ-centred way of life was so different that it made his colleague examine his own values. It can't have been easy to keep committed to Jesus while being targeted day in and day out.

I've known something of this kind of rejection myself. When I was a student at photographic school my fellow students mocked me for my photo-essay on the Christmas story. When I was a postgraduate student doing youth and community work studies a group of students tried to dissect my faith in an intense group dynamics session. When I was at theological college some criticized me because of my evangelical theology, and said I was 'too heavenly minded and no earthly good'.

These experiences did hurt. Looking back, I wish someone had warned me that I might face this undercurrent of opposition even in a so-called 'Christian' country. This kind of sarcasm is wearing and can take the cutting edge off our witness. It can make us want to compromise our values in order to be accepted. Such is the cost of an everyday commitment to Christ.

One of my political heroes was the late Gordon Wilson, who was accorded the highest honour in the Republic of Ireland by being made a Senator. This was a remarkable achievement when you know that he was a Protestant from Enniskillen. Few will forget how he and his daughter were buried under the rubble of a high wall after a huge IRA bomb exploded during the Remembrance Day Parade in his sleepy rural town.

Tragically his daughter died, but the day after the bombing Gordon went on national television appealing for calm and seeking to find a way to forgive. I once spent a cold November morning with him, walking by the river at Enniskillen. He told me that he had run a draper's shop in the High Street there for much of his working life. The tragedy of the bombing which killed his daughter was never a source of bitterness to him. He determined that through the power of Christ he would turn his personal heartbreak to good. He told me about his secret meetings with IRA and UDA leaders, and how he'd tried to persuade both sides to stop the killing and to lay down their arms. He risked his life on a number of occasions to find a means of reconciliation between those who considered themselves at war.

His commitment to Christ was the driving force behind his quest for peace. Surrender to Christ took him away from seeking retribution and turned him towards seeking reconciliation and redemption.

Gordon was someone who implemented his surrender to Christ in real and tangible ways. He did it in the way he lived, the way he loved and the way he risked his life to bring peace.

What shocked me was Gordon's honest admission that those secret negotiations, carried out in dark and hidden places, were not the most difficult aspect to his work or the most significant cost of his commitment. 'No,' he said, his voice wavering, 'the biggest cost has been the way I've been treated by former friends. Now, they cross the street rather than talk to me. To them, I'm a traitor.'

Gordon Wilson knew rejection because of his Christian commitment to reconciliation. He met with an undercurrent of opposition because he tried to interpret the Christian faith in his daily life.

No one warned me that surrender to Christ could lead to rejection like this. No one explained that if you seek to win others for Christ you may become the butt of humour. No one told me that if you go public about your faith, make a stand on some ethical issue, say 'no' to backhanders, or tell the truth even when it hurts, you may well be rejected.

If you read your Bible on the train, speak about Jesus in the staffroom or invite your friends to church, you'll soon discover that some will want to keep their distance from you. If you stand up for Jesus you may well find yourself standing alone. Sadly, no one warned me about this. And no one told me that just occasionally, I might meet this kind of resistance in the church itself. It was a huge disappointment to me to discover that some of those who I thought were 'on the same side' were so sceptical of Christian commitment, spirituality and evangelism.

Some Christians in the church have suffered bitter criticism for their orthodox biblical views, sarcasm about their prayer life and condemnation for their evangelism. I have met Christians who have been deeply hurt by this kind of attitude in the life of the local church.

As an evangelical Christian I have experienced this myself. I have received spiteful letters, seen committee resolutions and heard whispers of poisoned gossip. Sometimes it's been really difficult to handle. In one large committee the members were asked to form groups of three. They were invited to make a list of the things they disliked about my ministry. One from each group shouted out items from their discussion, while a composite list was scrawled onto a whiteboard. The main objection appeared to be concern about my practice of calling people forward at the close of meetings to commit their lives to Christ.

It was a meeting which resolved that I could only preach if I was in possession of a form signed in triplicate by regional and national members of the denomination. It was a restriction not imposed on any other Christian minister in the country.

I remember the long ride home on the top of a London bus, and the deep rejection which I felt. I will never forget how my prayer partner arrived at my house to pray with me, and how he encouraged me to 'keep on keeping on' no matter what form the opposition might take. Sometimes my commitment to Jesus has been costly. It has set me at odds with my friends, made me unpopular with the powerful, excluded me from the in crowd and put me out in the cold, even in the life of the church. When we surrender to Jesus we offer up our popularity. When we say, 'OK, Jesus, I'm willing to take up the cross and follow you, wherever, whatever,' it can lead to tough times.

Paul knew the pain of rejection like this. He was working among the Jewish community in Corinth when he testified that Jesus was the Messiah. So they '... opposed Paul and became abusive ...' (Acts 18:6).

It must have been hard for him to be rejected by his own people, but he had a beautiful vision of Jesus saying, 'Do not be afraid; keep on speaking, do not be silent. For I am with you ...' (Acts 18:9-10). In his lonely isolation Paul discovered that Jesus was still with him.

The Christian life is often difficult, and the journey of discipleship can take us through challenging times. Our commitment to Jesus may lead to trouble, opposition and suffering. He doesn't always take us out of the situation – but he promises that he will provide us with the strength to survive it.

Disappointments

I ran out of Westminster Central Hall and hailed a passing taxi. I was devastated. The committee inside, after only a few moments of debate, had consigned eighteen months' work to the bin.

By a vote of 13–9 a project to which I was passionately committed was rejected, and there was to be no right of appeal. We had faced committee after committee and overcome hurdle after hurdle – but now it was all wasted and I was deeply disappointed. I climbed into the taxi and sank back into the corner of the seat as we made the slow and frustrating journey to Euston. I raced across the mezzanine and boarded the train to Preston with only minutes to spare. As the train gathered speed I gazed out of the window in a kind of stupor. Soon the city sprawl was gone and the fields and trees flowed by. I mentally replayed the brief encounter in the committee room, wondering if I could have said something which might have changed the outcome. Tears filled my eyes. I couldn't believe that so much I'd hoped for would never be accomplished. It was a horrendous journey. There were endless delays, a missed connection, and a growing unease that I might not reach Barrow in time for the evening service. It was nearly dark by the time I reached the city, and it took another frantic taxi-ride to reach the church in time.

Throughout that journey I was convinced that the will of God had been thwarted. I believed that the mission centre at the heart of London that I had envisaged could make a major contribution to evangelism in the capital. I've never discovered what kind of church politics was active in that committee, who influenced whom, or what was whispered behind closed doors. All I know is that the building I had plans for was never used for the purposes my opponents specified.

A year later, when my ministry had been relocated and we had started to build an arts centre in a different part of London, the site still remained unused. It was offered to me again, but it was too late. I had relocated my staff, family and ministry once in twelve months and it was just not practical to do it again. This was a bitter experience and one which made me question how God's will is played out in the corridors of church power.

On that momentous decision day I arrived in Barrow just as the service was about to begin. I walked in the door and followed the choir into the packed church for the start of the Eucharist. When I got up to preach I was still wrestling with the pain and turmoil of the day's events, and felt like giving the sermon a miss. But when the time came for me to make the appeal, I found that in some way I was talking to myself. The challenge of total surrender which I was laying before the congregation was something that I needed to hear again myself. As I knelt at the communion table, with tears rolling down my cheeks, I realized that what really mattered in my life was knowing the Lord. I laid my work, my plans and my ministry before him again. I looked at the bread and wine and remembered what love he has for me, and knew again that he was the mainspring of my ministry.

Years later I still look back at the decision which that committee reached and feel that they may have misread the will of God. Even now I can't help but wonder what might have been if just two people had voted a different way. Even now I wonder how the will of God is played out in some of the policies formed by ecclesiastical bodies which I have never agreed with or begun to understand.

Sometimes I have been so convinced of the rightness of a way forward that I have dared to take on the powers that be in the hope of persuading them to change their mind.

When I was convinced of the vision to start an event called Easter People, a holiday convention which has touched the lives of tens of thousands of people over nearly twenty years, there was a great deal of scepticism in 'church headquarters'. No less than five national committees turned down the proposal, and without their support I could not proceed.

I arrived at my friend's farm for Christmas feeling dejected and despondent. When I explained the situation to Richard he asked that we kneel and commit the idea to the Lord. When that was done he said, 'Now, go and ask the five committees again.'

That's what I did, and to my amazement all five changed their vote and gave Easter People their blessing. It was a sober reminder that sometimes God's will can be delayed or even thwarted, and that sometimes we need to press on, even when others stand in the way. We may not understand some of the disappointments and confusions of our lives, particularly when they seem to be the result of the actions of fellow Christians.

I have known at least six young people who were turned down for Christian ministry, when I felt that each was genuinely called and capable. Some of them have taken that 'no' as an opportunity to develop other forms of vocation, and have made outstanding contributions to social work, business or education. Others have struggled with the disappointment of that rejection. It has halted their development and even scarred their lives.

Coping with disappointment as a Christian is part of the challenge of commitment. When we miss God's 'best' for us, either through our own stupidity or the failure of others, we need to look out for God to reveal the next exciting chapter of his plan. Even if it is plan T! Like George Verwer, I think I'm long past plan A, but he's still guiding me after many failures and many frustrations along the way. No one ever explained to me that when one door closes we should press on to try all the other doors until we find one that's right for us. No one told me that we sometimes need a 'bloody-minded' persistence to keep on trying doors, and that this is an important aspect of Christian commitment.

If you wear the yoke of obedience, you put him in the driving seat and trust that he will guide. You must cling on to this, even when you feel you've missed the turning. God's will has never been as clear to comprehend or as easy to obey as I was led to believe. Obedience to God has been one of the most painful and costly aspects of my Christian discipleship.

No matter what happens to us, or what is done to us, we mustn't lose this sense of his providential guidance along the way. Richard Wurmbrand underwent terrible suffering and torture during his imprisonment in Romania under Communism. Many of his bones were broken, including four vertebrae in his back. His body was carved in a dozen places, and he had eighteen holes cut and burnt into his flesh. He had to strip to the waist before one US Senate committee to prove what torture he'd endured. Yet in his powerful book *Tortured for Christ* he could still write

> If the heart is cleansed by the love of Jesus Christ, and if the heart loves him, one can resist all tortures. God will not judge us according to how much we endured, but how much we could love.

Occasionally I've been privileged to pastor those whose health posed big questions about the will of God. Once I spent a lot of time with a terminally ill businessman who was seeking to decipher God's will in his traumatic cancer treatment.

'I've always sensed the will of God,' he said. 'There have been many signposts all down the years, and I've always felt that I was travelling the track God had directed me down. But now, sick as I am, I feel I've run out of signs.' He died shortly afterwards, and I felt that perhaps God's last signpost for him had simply pointed 'Home'.

Our final act of obedience to God's will is in the journey to death and the life beyond. It's what the Salvationists call 'promotion to glory', a phrase that reminds us that even in heaven there will still be things to do. We need to plan today with an awareness of life's transience and fragility. If we are only living for this life we're forgetting that the best is yet to be. James gives us a stern warning on this subject:

> Now listen, you who say, 'Today or tomorrow we will go to this or that city, spend a year there, carry on business and make money.' Why, you do not even know what will happen tomorrow. What is your life? You are a mist that appears for a little while and then vanishes. Instead, you ought to say, 'If it is the Lord's will, we will live and do this or that' (Jas. 4:13-15).

So often we organize our future according to our own mortal worldview. We plan out our lives in the Lord's service without even asking what he wants. We choose the opportunities that suit us best without submitting ourselves to his purposes. We turn away when we don't agree with the way he's leading.

Every one of us who wants to find the will of God must offer our life to him and accept that in all the confusing options before us, he is the only one who knows the best way ahead. A contemporary paraphrase of James' instruction about guidance has really helped me. It reads

So let God work his will in you. Yell a loud *no* to the Devil and watch him scamper. Say a quiet *yes* to God and he'll be there in no time. Quit dabbling in sin. Purify your inner life. Quit playing the field. Hit bottom, and cry your eyes out. The fun and games are over. Get serious, really serious. Get down on your knees before the Master; it's the only way you'll get on your feet (Jas. 4:7-10, The Message).

The Christian plod

In the early days of my Christian discipleship I saw 'commitment' and 'surrender' as mountain top experiences. Looking back, however, those high moments of Christian experience weren't always translated into my normal everyday life.

No one taught me that commitment is much more than a series of emotional highs. It has to be worked out in everyday routine and implemented in mundane work situations. The Christian life is made up of a delicate weave of different decisions, each of which is submitted to the will of God. Sometimes our failure in the smallest of these decisions can affect the whole pattern of our lives so that it becomes flawed and disjointed. Surrender to Jesus needs to be worked out in the nitty-gritty of life and in ways that we don't even bother to talk about. When we start out on the Christian life many of us have the kind of faith that can seemingly move mountains. The possibilities of Christian ministry stretch out before us. Our prayers are alive and we constantly look to see how the Lord will answer them. Our faith matches the classic definition found in Hebrews 11:1: 'Faith is being sure of what we hope for and certain of what we do not see.'

After a while, however, it's easy for the pressures of life and ministry to drag us down and for the joy we once knew to evaporate. Disillusion can wrap itself around our thinking, and we can become half-hearted in the life of prayer. I have seen this happen in the lives of many leaders who are heavily involved in church life. I have met youth leaders who have slogged on year after year but have grown tired and fed up. Enthusiasm has dwindled and faith has become dull.

Some ministers have faced entrenched attitudes and petty traditionalism for years on end, and a deep sense of disillusion has taken root. They've become fed up with everything and everyone, their ministry has become a burden and they've become too exhausted to pray.

Once an older minister told me that I was trying to do too much, too soon. He showed me that I'd been setting targets for myself which were not the Lord's, and that I'd been racing towards goals that he was not asking me to reach. It was a solemn warning, and I readjusted my workload as soon as I could. Whatever sphere of Christian service we commit ourselves to, we can be tempted to shoulder burdens which Christ has not asked us to bear. Our Christianity can become works and not faith. We can lose our grip on Jesus.

Life's pressures and demands can grind us down, and the last thing we feel like doing is to keep going. Over the years, however, I've become convinced that there is a devotion to duty, a commitment to service and a surrender to finish the task which is at the heart of true Christian commitment. We may want to run away from all those tedious, boring and depressing jobs which are part of Christian service, but accomplishing them is integral to fulfilling our Christian commitment. At times like this, commitment is not so much about emotional response as about grit determination.

Once, when I was on a hike with my two sons, we took a wrong turn. I don't know how it happened, because the nature trail we'd been following was clearly signposted and the pathway should have been easy to follow.

We must have been distracted and turned right instead of left – my navigation skills are not very good at the best of times. Before long we were completely lost and wondered if we should press on or turn back. My sons looked at me in desperation – they'd been in this situation with me before! We pressed on, but the path got narrower and narrower until I had to carry my youngest son through a bed of stinging nettles. It was obvious that we had left the beaten track and turned off into the wilderness. I was tempted to give up, but I knew that I simply had to 'plod on' until we reached our destination.

Many Christians are exhausted by the journey of Christian ministry. Some look for a quick-acting spiritual pick-me-up, and if they don't find it they become deeply disillusioned. I've found, however, that I'm most likely to rediscover the Lord's renewed blessing and a fresh anointing on my life as I simply continue with the daily plod of discipleship.

It is in the plod of Christian fellowship, the plod of a disciplined prayer time, the plod of attendance at worship, and the plod of continuing commitment to Jesus that I discover new blessing. The Christian plod may not seem very exciting, but it's the surest way out of the wilderness. It's only as we continue to serve the Lord through thick and thin that we find he is still working in our lives.

It is in the hard graft of service, the discipline of surrender and the daily plod of commitment that we give the Lord the opportunity to break into our lives and to bring us back to him.

At the heart of the 'Christian plod' is a covenant between ourselves and the Lord which is the sure foundation for our faith. It is a covenant which we need to remake again and again as the years go by. In August 1755 John Wesley introduced a simple order of service known as the Covenant service. It was a powerful time of rededication, and it quickly became a popular event in Methodist fellowships.

Methodists all over the world still hold annual Covenant services and they still use the same basic outline prepared by John Wesley.

The Covenant prayer takes the 'ifs' and 'buts' out of Christian commitment and describes explicitly how to live this 'Christian plod'. It's a covenant which can seem harder to make as the years go by. It's not that my commitment to Jesus is any the less, but that the cost of this commitment grows more real as time goes by. Wesley's prayer consists of a number of poignant phrases.

'*I am no longer my own, but yours.*' Only as we resign ourselves completely to his will can we discover his purpose for our lives. Life is not something to cling on to, but something to be given and shared.

'*Put me to what you will, rank me with whom you will.*' Wesley's covenant promise doesn't say, 'Put me to what I feel I'm capable of.' Even now, after many years in the ministry, I still find myself approaching situations which I don't know how to handle. Sometimes I have stood outside the home of a bereaved family not knowing what to say, or have waited in church vestries feeling inadequate about my preaching. But in submission I have discovered that God could use me, even when my best wasn't good enough.

'*Put me to doing, put me to suffering.*' Whatever God's plan for our lives might involve, we should be ready to accept it and to live it for his glory. If our faith collapses when we face suffering, it can't be real. Time and again I've seen Christians use experiences of suffering for the glory of God and, even in the most awful circumstances, find a radiant peace.

'Let me be employed for you or laid aside for you.' Activists like myself find these words some of the hardest to say. Many of us who enjoy a hectic lifestyle and ever-changing opportunities for service dread the very thought of stopping. Part of saying 'anything' to the Lord is a willingness to be laid aside and a recognition that it's God's work and not our own.

'Exalted for you or brought low for you.' Once I came across a sign in a church vestry which read, 'You can't convince people that you're a good preacher and that Christ is a wonderful Saviour!' It can be difficult to keep walking the path of genuine humility, but in all our work for him the only thing that really matters is that he is glorified.

'Let me be full, let me be empty; let me have all things, let me have nothing.' Whether we own a lot or very little, we must realize that we are holding these things in trust from him. When we learn to share what we have and to give to others without holding back, we'll find true joy. Our aim in life shouldn't be to own more, but to share more.

'I freely and wholeheartedly yield all things to your pleasure and disposal.' The starting point for all Christian discipleship must be the death of our old selves. The clay must lose its old shape if the Potter is to work with us. If we allow him to mould our lives we will discover that his will for us is perfect.

No one told me that if I was feeling restless and disillusioned, I simply needed to return to my covenant with Christ and the discipline of this Christian plod.

For in giving myself to this everyday discipline I am, in effect, giving my life back to him. When Hudson Taylor was on board the old steamship *Lammermuir* bound for China, he felt both physically and emotionally at the end. The boat went through a terrible storm, and for sixteen days the wind and waves pounded it. The passengers and crew prepared to die. At this all-time low Taylor wrote

> Burdens, such as I never before sustained, responsibilities such as I had not hitherto incurred, and sorrows – compared with which all my past sorrows were light, have been part of my experience ... But I trust I have in some feeble measure learned more of the blessed truth that – 'sufficient is his arm alone and our defence is sure'.

Christian discipleship can be difficult whatever your age, and the society in which we live can be very unsympathetic. Those of us who are committed to the Lord face many pressures as we serve Christ and try to live lives worthy of our calling. In remaining faithful to the task, we also can discover that 'sufficient is his arm alone and our defence is sure'.

When I say the words 'I am the bread of life. He who comes to me will never go hungry' (Jn. 6:35) when distributing bread at the Eucharist and I look at the different hands outstretched to receive, I am often deeply moved. Black hands and white hands; some wrinkled with age, others young and smooth. Hands gnarled by work. Hands twisted with arthritis. Hands open to receive. The hands of those who pass through days of loneliness and hardship. As I place bread in each hand I am symbolizing the fact that Christ's presence will be bread for the journey. And as they rise from the Lord's Table, they go out with the strength of the Bread of Life. He alone can give the grace sufficient for every need.

Sometimes I would have liked the Lord to have changed things or to have taken me away from difficult situations, but it hasn't happened. The situation remains the same, the problem doesn't change, the difficult relationships are still to be faced. And yet, somehow, everything is different. Through the power of Jesus, I've been changed within, I've been strengthened and I've been renewed. I've discovered the empowering presence of Christ with me in the situation.

Committed to Jesus

I stood in quiet reverence. I had reached the destination of my journey. The long hours of travel and the many weeks of preparation were behind me. I was standing beside the Garden Tomb in Jerusalem. This spot had become the focal point for my travels, the place where I would pause to remember the events of that first Easter morning. 'Come,' said the elderly guide, 'step inside and see – the tomb is empty.'

I stepped into the cave and turned to look out to the beautiful garden beyond. In my mind I reran the events of Easter morning. I saw Mary Magdalene approaching the tomb with the spices in her hand. I saw her surprise at finding the body gone. I heard her cry of despair to the gardener: 'They have taken my Lord away, and I don't know where they have put him' (Jn. 20:13). But this was no gardener. This was the risen Lord. Christ had overcome the power of death and opened the way to eternal life. Christ had risen triumphant over the power of evil, and anticipated the final victory.

Christ had defeated the power of suffering, and risen victorious to be our source of renewing strength. Jesus Christ had risen from the dead!

I knew again that he was the source of my faith, my ministry and my life. No one told me that when my commitment wears thin and my surrender is actually 'no surrender', I must retrace my steps to the empty tomb: I must refocus on Jesus. Spend time with him again. Discover what he wants of me. Find in him the strength to do it. Allow him to grow bigger in my life while my work grows smaller. It's time to rediscover the Saviour who is my friend, the One to whom I am committed. The One who calls me to a life of discipleship.

3

What they didn't tell me about intimacy with Christ

Regrets

One of my regrets is that I spent so many years of my Christian journey with a dearth of understanding about the spiritual life, and a shallow experience of Christian spirituality. I lived too many years as a spiritual pauper, and the quality of my Christian life and experience has suffered because of it. I fear that many new Christians continue to be launched into this spiritually impoverished form of Christianity.

When I first became a Christian I was introduced to Christian spirituality as being a 'quiet time', which was five minutes or more spent in 'devotions' each day. This 'quiet time' consisted of a Bible reading, a short explanatory passage and a 'prayer list' of petitions and intercessions to bring to Christ each day.

Whilst I recognize that such an introduction to the Christian life was better than nothing, it gave me only a very rudimentary understanding of what Christian spirituality is all about. Because I thought that this was 'it', I saw no reason to look for anything more.

As a result, my journey towards intimacy with Christ took a lot longer than it should have done. Sadly,

I thought that I had arrived – when in fact I hadn't even started the journey. I'm convinced that countless other Christians are living out their days with only the vaguest understanding of what Christian spirituality is all about. As a result they are missing out on the most enriching element of the Christian life.

One of the most encouraging aspects of church renewal today is a rediscovery of our heritage of Christian spirituality. There is a growing commitment to prayer and a new hunger for God. Among many younger Christians there seems a very real hunger for intimacy with God and a much greater sense of commitment to the life of prayer.

Access

In the Old Testament the focus of devotion was the Temple. The high walls of the Court of the Gentiles, the Court of Israel, the Court of Jewish men and the Court of the priests each seem to have been designed to keep those of inferior status shut out.

At the centre of it all was the Holy of Holies, with its golden roof which reflected the scorching sun. Only one person could enter that holy place, and that was the High Priest. He could only enter on one day each year, the Day of Atonement. Access to God was strictly by invitation only.

I was in a West End cinema at a press showing of the movie *The Passion of the Christ* when I discovered that I was sitting next to a reviewer from the *Daily Mail*. When the dramatic scene of the crucifixion appeared on screen, we watched as Jesus gave up his soul. As he did so, there was a slow dissolve to the dramatic events at the Temple. The thick curtain covering the

Holy Place was mysteriously torn in two, the earth shook, the tombs opened, and a new era began.

The journalist nudged me and whispered, 'What a work of fiction. Mel Gibson's imagination is running wild!' I turned and replied, 'Maybe you should read your Bible before you write your review.'

The movie was faithful in its portrayal of the biblical story. Matthew records that in the moment when Jesus cried out with a loud voice and gave up his spirit, 'the curtain of the temple was torn in two from top to bottom. The earth shook and the rocks split' (Mt. 27:51). I believe that in that instant something spiritually significant occurred. The era in which the walls shut us out, the curtains excluded us and the doors were locked against us was over once and for all.

I wish I had grasped this important truth at the start of my Christian journey. For many years I lived as though prayer depended on me 'gaining access' to the presence of God. Devotion was a matter of effort rather than grace. Spirituality was about what I did rather than enjoying what Jesus had done for me.

Once a Christian called Ros worked in my office. Her husband worked for the Royal Family and from time to time one of the officials at Buckingham Palace would phone to invite Ros to 'make up the numbers' at some special royal banquet or dinner party at the Palace. These requests became so common that Ros left her beautiful ball gown hanging on my office door 'just in case'. After she'd been for dinner with the Queen, the next day we'd all be eagerly waiting to hear whom she'd met, what was said and what they'd eaten. I think we all walked a foot taller because one of our team had been elevated to such a position. We had a friend in high places. We had access to the highest place in the land through someone we knew, and someone who knew us.

In Jesus Christ I have a friend in a much higher place than Buckingham Palace. I am no longer shut out. I have a Saviour who knows me and who loves me and who welcomes me into the spiritual realm, the highest place of all. 'Therefore, since we have a great high priest who has gone through the heavens, Jesus the Son of God, let us hold firmly to the faith we profess' (Heb. 4:14).

Access to this holy place is the starting point for my spiritual journey. Because he died on Calvary and 'went through the heavens', he opened the way for me into the presence of God. He gave me open access to the holiest place of all. No one ever explained to me that intimacy with Christ begins here, or that at any time I had the right to approach the One who is at the apex of all things. No one helped me to understand that this privilege is an integral part of the Christian lifestyle. I never realized that prayer is simply about being with 'my friend in high places'.

As the years go by I want to linger in this holy place more and more. I want to be present with him in that holy place as an essential part of my everyday life. Nothing can overwhelm me when I am seated there with Christ. Paul knew exactly what this means when he wrote to the Ephesians

> And God raised us up with Christ and seated us with him in the heavenly realms in Christ Jesus, in order that in the coming ages he might show the incomparable riches of his grace, expressed in his kindness to us in Christ Jesus (Eph. 2:6-7).

This means that as I live my ordinary existence on earth I can live in another dimension, too. Stephen Motyer unpacked this when he wrote in *Discovering Ephesians*

We are not really in two places at all, because the heavenly realms intersect with this world like the light which falls outside the visible spectrum. Ultra-violet light is really there, and can affect us a lot. On a hot day, my white skin becomes red and sore. But I can't actually see the light which does this to me. Similarly, we human beings live on two planes at the same time, the spiritual and the physical, each as 'real' as the other. We need to learn to live in Christ in both sides of our existence, earthly and heavenly.

The distance between my life here and my life with him has diminished with the years, so that movement between the two is now an integral part of my faith. The curtain of mystery between the endless pressure of my waking days and the awesome silence of eternity has been opened. I can move from here to there in the busiest of days and in the most secular of situations. No one ever told me that this might be possible.

For me, devotion has become less about doing and more about being. Prayer is about moving beyond a life of transience and into a place of transcendence. Christian spirituality is about living through the schedules of human existence alongside the timeless wonder of eternity.

This understanding has enriched my life and is woven into the fabric of who I am. Now I really know that all may come and enter the Holy Place. Nothing is required but a heartfelt desire to be with him.

Spirituality

Over the last five years I have been studying and writing about New Age spirituality in order to understand what so many people are looking for today.

W.H. Clark, writing in *The Psychology of Religion*, described spirituality as 'the inner experience of the individual when he senses a Beyond, especially as evidenced by the effect of this experience on his behaviour when he actively attempts to harmonize his life with the Beyond.' Many ordinary people are searching for the life beyond, using whale music and crystals, ley lines and chakras, massage and meditation. For some, this quest to connect with the fragile forces of the earth leads them to green spirituality and devotion of Gaia. I believe that these activities are misplaced and flawed.

I respect those involved in this movement who have a heartfelt desire to discover the 'beyond'. They spend a lot of money and a great deal of personal energy in looking for it. Their hunger for a spiritual dimension to life is to be highly commended. Sadly, it's a hunger often missing in mature Christians. Many churchgoers appear to be satisfied with their limited understanding of spirituality and express no desire for anything more. Research indicates that many Christians feel disillusioned with the spirituality of church worship services and are disappointed with the level of their own spiritual experience. After lecturing on this subject in different parts of the world I am astonished at how many Christians are willing to talk about this dissatisfaction. Sadly, most of them don't seem to want to give the time or energy required to discover the rich heritage of Christian spirituality.

Like me, many Christians were never introduced to the riches of Christian mysticism, the wisdom of the desert fathers or the Christian practices of meditation and contemplation. Sadly, some Christians have written off Christian spirituality without ever understanding what it is or seeking the personal renewal which it can bring.

A generation of Christians has grown up in the church but has been denied the riches of their spiritual inheritance. They are functioning without the personal joy of union with Christ. Christian mysticism doesn't need the props of the New Age movement, for it rests on the biblical truth that the way to God is already wide open. Too few of us, however, have dared to linger in 'the holy place'.

If you ever have the opportunity to visit the ruins of the ancient city of Ephesus, I'd recommend that you go. This site is near the Mediterranean coast of modern-day Turkey, and it's one of the great archaeological wonders of the world.

As I strolled through the ancient ruins of the main street in the intense summer heat, I was staggered to discover just how many shrines, religious buildings and 'sacred spaces' the archaeologists have uncovered in the religious quarter of this ancient city.

Ephesus was a centre for alternative spiritualities. Paul stayed there for two years, teaching and preaching about the joy of a relationship with Christ. Into this dreadful place with its temple brothels and Emperor-worship cults, where sacrificial ceremonies and a heady mix of weird and wonderful religious rites were practised openly day by day, Paul preached about the authenticity of Christian spirituality.

Last year I led a communion service in the ruins of the ancient church at Ephesus, which dates back to earliest Christian times. As I broke the bread, I thought of that great bustling city where Paul taught, and remembered his prayer for this home of competing spiritualities.

I pray that out of his glorious riches he may strengthen you with power through his Spirit in your inner being, so that Christ may dwell in your hearts through faith (Eph. 3:16-17).

Paul taught that access to the 'beyond' was not through the peculiar activities of Ephesian spirituality but through a living relationship with Christ. 'In him and through faith in him we may approach God with freedom and confidence' (Eph. 3:12).

It was many years before I fully grasped what Paul meant when he talked of approaching God 'with freedom and confidence'. But now I know that each and every day I can walk through an open door into the holiest place of all. When I started out on the Christian journey my theology of prayer was more about disciplines to be learnt and things to do. My devotional life was shaped by Christian 'product' rather than biblical understanding. In recent years, however, I have come to see that no Bible notes, meditation CDs, praise tapes, liturgies or prayer books are actually necessary for access to the holy place. In fact, these very 'resources' can become an end rather than a means. They can focus me on the words and concepts of men rather than on the joyous presence of the Living Christ.

Whenever I am travelling through the United States I try to meet a friend called Ben Campbell Johnson. He is about twenty years older and forty years wiser than me. When I stay at his lovely home in Atlanta he often takes me on a morning jog. His advanced years and my lack of stamina mean this exercise regime gives us ample time to talk and to pray!

Ben was for many years the Professor of Spirituality at Columbia Theological Seminary in Atlanta. With his understanding of the human spirit and his knowledge of Christian spirituality, these morning 'walks' are rich times of sharing. He, too, looks back down the track of his Christian life with regret for the years he lived in spiritual poverty. In *Confessing a Life* he wrote

> To live with material poverty is one thing, but spiritual poverty deprives the human spirit more deeply. Lacking knowledge of God casts us into the wilderness of a strange and barren land. If only I could have known you, felt your power around me and your presence within me, how different would those early years have been. ... How impoverished and empty was my spiritual life, O God.

On our morning walks he has challenged me to look for a deeper walk with Christ myself, and I recognize that I still have much to discover. I know that as I reach mid-life and beyond, I will need this deeper understanding of the presence of Christ more and more. If I haven't learnt how to contemplate and meditate before I die, I might find heaven something of a struggle! Regrettably, my early understanding of Christian spirituality was very much discipline-focused and guilt-ridden. Much of what I learnt about prayer turned me off and meant that I dismissed the riches of Christian spirituality before I'd even discovered what they were.

Like Ben, I wish that someone had enthused me about intimacy with Christ at the very start of my journey. In my fifties I'm still in the early days of discovering more about the mystery of God's presence, but what I've already experienced drives me forward to look for more. One day I hope that I will find what the theologian Richard of St Victor wrote about in his twelfth-century book *Of the Four Degrees*, when he said

> The third degree of love is when the mind of man is ravished into the abyss of divine light, so that the soul,

having forgotten all outward things, is altogether unaware of itself, and passes out completely into its God.

Presence

My favourite account of the Resurrection is the story of the walk to Emmaus. As the evening shadows lengthened, two disciples met a stranger who walked beside them. They were confused and sad, and invited the stranger to join them for supper.

They didn't know that the Lord was there, and they had no evidence of his presence, but as he broke the bread, the scales fell from their eyes and they saw. Of course, he had been there all along. They just hadn't recognized him. No one told me, when I first became a Christian, that he was still with me, even when I couldn't see him, and that he'd always accompany me on the journey, even when I didn't know that he was there. No one taught me that his presence is not something I have to strive for, but a rich gift to be received and enjoyed as the journey continues. I've discovered that even when I'm not in a praising mood, he's there. And even when I'm trying to live my life without him, he's still around, patiently waiting. The great Christian leader St Augustine struggled to find faith, but once he became a believer his insights were profound. He knew this 'abiding presence of Christ', and he suffered for having lived so long without it. He wrote

Late have I loved thee, O beauty so ancient and so new; late have I loved thee. For behold thou wert within me, and I outside, and I sought thee outside, and in my unloveliness fell upon those lovely things that thou hast made. Thou wert with me, and I was not with thee. I

> was kept from thee by these things, yet had they not
> been in thee, they would not have been at all. Thou didst
> call and cry to me to break open my deafness, and thou
> didst send forth thy beams and shine upon me and chase
> away my blindness. Thou didst breathe fragrance upon
> me, and I drew in my breath and do now pant for thee.
> I tasted thee, and now hunger and thirst for thee. Thou
> didst touch me, and I have burned for thy peace.

For me, this discovery of the presence of Christ in the
whole of life has been profoundly liberating. The true
joy of Christian spirituality is in finding him wherever
I am.

I once had a very traumatic experience under the sea.
It happened during my first and, as it turned out, my
last attempt at scuba diving. I was given a few minutes
of instruction by a diver on a Spanish beach and told
that I must swim underwater beside him. Under no
circumstances was I to come to the surface without him
by my side.

This was all very well until he swam at such speed
that gradually his flippers disappeared in a cloud of
bubbles ahead of me and I was left there under the sea,
feeling all alone. Remembering his stern instruction that
I must not surface, I descended a couple more metres to
the ocean floor and stood there, wondering what to do
and waiting. I was there for some considerable time.

I learnt later that my instructor went to the surface,
hailed the diving launch and proceeded to circle the bay
looking for my bubbles. That wait on the ocean floor
was one of the longest waits of my life. But right there,
deep below the surface of the sea, with fish swimming
all around me, a verse from the Bible popped into my
head and I found myself repeating it over and over
again.

Where can I go from your Spirit? Where can I flee from your presence? If I go up to the heavens, you are there; if I make my bed in the depths, you are there (Ps. 139:7-8).

I had discovered that even there, alone, desperate and close to the 'world of the dead', he was with me. Jesus said to his disciples, 'Remain in me, and I will remain in you' (Jn. 15:4). The abiding presence of Christ is the place to make your dwelling and the place to call home. Dean Farrar wrote

'Oh, where is the sea?' the fishes cried,
as they swam the crystal waters through.
'We have heard from of old of the ocean tide,
and we long to look on the waters blue.
The wise ones speak of the infinite sea –
Oh, who can tell us if such there be?'

The fish couldn't reach the sea because it already enveloped them, they couldn't see it because they were already immersed in it, and they couldn't find it because it was already sustaining them.

Over the years I have realized that I am living a life immersed in the presence of God, but am often too busy to notice it. Whilst being hungry for more of him, I haven't recognized the richness of his presence which surrounds me and sustains me on every side.

No one explained that all I had to do was to stop and practise the presence of God. For his presence is everywhere. Paul told the Colossians

Since, then, you have been raised with Christ, set your hearts on things above, where Christ is seated at the right hand of God. Set your minds on things above, not on earthly things (Col. 3:1-2).

No one told me that experiencing God's presence is at the very heart of Christianity or that this sense of 'presence' is available wherever we may be. When I have known it, I have discovered one of the greatest treasures of Christianity. My experience of 'presence' has become more and more important to me with the passing years and the experiences of my life. His presence is part of my everyday experience and I find myself more and more aware of it. It surrounds me like a sea, and sustains me in a way that helps me face the storms of life.

His presence lifts me above the endless pressures of the everyday to glimpse a greater purpose for my life. In moments of rejection and pain it sustains me emotionally, and in days of sickness it provides me with a strength greater than my own.

My life is enriched by an ever-present friend who brings an extra dimension to my human experience. He gives me a sense of my uniqueness as an individual and an insight into my destiny. This was not something that I was introduced to in my early Christian life; it's something which has grown with the joys and heartaches of the years.

When I last visited Kenya, I heard the people in the villages still singing a Christian song which I had first heard there when I visited nearly thirty years ago. The men sang 'Where do you live?' and the women replied 'I live in Christ.' The question and answer are repeated until they joyfully sing together, 'For there's no condemnation in my heart.' I now know what they're singing about. This sense of living in Christ and of abiding in him is at the centre of my Christian experience. Better late than never!

Connection

The Celtic Christians were serving God in an age which was in some ways similar to our own. Celtic paganism was the dominant force in society, and the Christians were trying to communicate their faith in a hostile environment. The beliefs and practices of the pagans were resonant with many aspects of the contemporary New Age movement. Both are characterized by a deep hunger for mysticism, a great reverence for the natural order and a desire to connect with the powerful forces of nature. My New Age friends talk a lot about their 'connection with all things'. They talk of the interconnectedness of everything and of the powers of Gaia which keep in tension the delicate balance of the eco-system.

The Celtic Christians have much to teach us about how to make Christianity relevant in an age such as this. The Celtic Christians did not look for the presence of God in man-made shrines or sanctuaries, for they believed that the presence of Christ infused all things everywhere. They sensed his presence in the power of the crashing surf, the music of the babbling spring, the mystery of the white-misted mountain and the dancing spray of the waterfall. They felt God in the soft refreshing rain, saw him in the colourful arch of the rainbow, and touched him in the wet dew of a new morning. The whole of the created order was their holy space. Their Christianity taught that Christ's promise to be with us was not just an experience of the heart. They believed that his presence imbued everything, and that wherever they were there was sacred space. They did not only know Christ in their spirit but also in the beautiful natural places that surrounded them. Their theology talked of a Creator who didn't just put it all in place and then walk away, but who continued to sustain and support his Creation. They worshipped a God whose power continued to hold in tension the delicate balances of the eco-system.

It's a tragedy that so much of our contemporary Christian experience has become locked up in words and buildings, for God intended his presence to permeate the whole world. Evangelical practice has majored on the presence of Christ within 'our hearts' when in fact he is everywhere and his Spirit is all around us. A poem by Joseph Mary Plunkett has really helped me to grasp this important truth personally:

I see his blood upon the rose
And in the stars the glory of his eyes,
His body gleams amid eternal snows,
His tears fall from the skies.
I see his face in every flower;
The thunder and the singing of the birds
Are but his voice – and carven by his power
Rocks are his written words.
All pathways by his feet are worn,
His strong heart stirs the ever-beating sea,
His crown of thorns is twined in every thorn,
His cross is every tree.

One of my heroes in the academic world of science and theology is Professor John Polkinghorne, whom I once had the privilege of hosting for tea at the Pizza Hut in Cambridge. I found our conversation quite challenging, as I failed GCSE physics, but I marvelled at his ability to put into simple words a view of the cosmic Christ who 'holds it all together', so that even I could understand. He said, 'He is the source of connection, the one whose creative act holds in tension the world-views of science, aesthetics, ethics and religion.'

Polkinghorne teaches that there is no divide between the sacred and the secular: Jesus Christ is in all, and Lord of all. We are connected to the One who is the source of connection of all things.

No one ever unpacked this kind of thinking for me when I first became a Christian, and I developed much of my Christian understanding in separate compartments clearly labelled 'sacred' and 'secular'. Over recent years I've tried to demolish these walls which keep God locked up in a religious box. There is a contemporary paraphrase of Colossians 1 which I love: it describes this sense of the interconnectedness of all things which has become such an important part of my spiritual experience in recent years:

> He was supreme in the beginning and – leading the resurrection parade – he is supreme in the end. From beginning to end he's there, towering far above everything, everyone. So spacious is he, so roomy, that everything of God finds its proper place in him without crowding. Not only that, but all the broken and dislocated pieces of the universe – people and things, animals and atoms – get properly fixed and fit together in vibrant harmonies, all because of his death, his blood that poured down from the Cross (Col. 1:17-20, The Message).

Silence

I've always known that Jesus was my Friend. I knew it as an infant when I heard the prayers of my mother at my bedside, and I learnt about it in Sunday school when I sang songs like 'Jesus, friend of little children'. What I didn't grasp was that this friendship is richer than any other, and I never understood the enormity of its power or the security of its constancy. Of course I knew what it was to trust a friend, to share with a friend and to know the affection and affirmation of a friend. It was a long time, however, before I began to realize that the friendship of Jesus is so much greater than any human friendship. His friendship is in a different dimension, it's at a deeper level, and it has a transforming power quite beyond any ordinary human relationship.

I once met a lecturer in philosophy when I was leading a Christian holiday in the South of France. He was one of the hundred or so campers sharing the same field. One of the rich experiences of leading holiday groups such as this is that you never know who you might be paddling with in the warm waters of the Mediterranean!

As we ambled along the seashore we talked about philosophy, and I soon found myself intellectually out of my depth. Then we talked about Christ, and the academic told me about his long and arduous journey to Christian discipleship. At last he said, 'Do you know why I became a Christian?' What followed was a great testimony to God's grace, in which he said, 'In all my study of philosophy I discovered that there was nothing in the teachings of the great philosophers which could cure my essential aloneness as a human being. Only Jesus could do that.'

The lecturer in philosophy was right. I can be surrounded by friends and feel alone. I can have rich relationships and still feel lonely. My friendship with Jesus, however, is of a different order. His friendship reaches to the core of my being and brings a security and constancy which promises, 'I will never leave you nor forsake you.' Teilhard de Chardin summed it up when he wrote

> Radiant Word, Blazing Power, you who mould the manifold so as to breathe your life into it, I pray you, lay on me your hands, powerful and considerate, omnipresent, which plunge into the depths of the totality of my being through all that is most profound.

Christ's friendship is soaked in a love which plumbs the depths of the totality of my being. It's a love through which my brokenness is healed, my worries are dissolved and my confusion resolved. It's a friendship which is 'powerful and considerate' and always omnipresent. It's a friendship which brings indescribable joy. It's a friendship enriched by the silence of eternity.

The coach roared as it climbed the steep hill beside the Sea of Galilee. Finally it reached the summit and turned into a lane beside the church. It was a quiet and beautiful place. My friends and I walked out onto the church veranda overlooking the Sea of Galilee. We stood gazing at the beauty of the rolling green hills reflected in the still blue waters of the lake. A thin mist in the distance gave an air of mystery to the scene. The stillness was almost tangible. Drifting from the church behind us came the muffled sound of singing. Time stood still. Jesus seemed so close. He was there. Here was the silence of eternity. It was there, on that same hillside, that Jesus said

> And when you pray, do not keep on babbling like pagans, for they think they will be heard because of their many words. Do not be like them, for your Father knows what you need before you ask him (Mt. 6:7-8).

No one told me about prayers without words when I first became a Christian. I was mentored into prayers of petition, prayers of intercession, prayers of repentance and prayers of adoration, but no one told me that sometimes words are unnecessary. In fact words can get in the way of the friendship which is nourished by silence.

Bishop Desmond Tutu understands this kind of prayer. He was one of the foremost Christian leaders who led the struggle against apartheid. Tutu grew up in the mining towns along the east coast of South Africa, and he came to prominence when he was awarded the 1984 Nobel Peace Prize for his work with the South African Council of Churches.

He said that the award was for those uprooted from their homes and 'dumped', as if they were rubbish. I once met him when he was preaching in Atlanta and I was deeply moved by the power of his simple message and the joy of his Resurrection faith at the height of the difficulties in South Africa. Years later I read a newspaper article in which he described the source of his passion for justice and his personal courage in such traumatic circumstances. He spoke of his relationship with Christ as 'a silence between friends', a silence which is deeper and richer than words can express. At the time of the interview he was struggling with prostate cancer and grieving over the death of his son. This 'silence between friends', he declared, was what gave him the inner strength to carry on. He wrote

> Most of us have had that experience where you sit with someone you are deeply fond of and you don't have to use words – you seem to communicate at a level you didn't know existed. When you sit quietly with God, you will find that the silence is a pregnant silence. It is not the absence of noise – it is something positive.

Like Tutu, I have discovered that my friendship with Jesus doesn't always need words. Sometimes it is

enough just to be with him. It's sufficient to know that
he is there and to bathe in the silence of his presence.
When I first became a Christian, no one explained just
how wonderful, how mystical and how rich this 'silence
between friends' could be. Even as I write, I sense the
power and reality of it. As the years go by, I long that
I might know it more.

The great Christian mystic Angela of Foligno (1248-
1309) knew this silence between friends. She wrote

> And when I looked, I beheld God who spake with me.
> But if thou seekest to know that which I beheld, I can tell
> thee nothing, save that I beheld a fullness and a clearness,
> and felt them within me so abundantly that I can in no
> wise describe it, nor give any likeness thereof.

Seasons

Those who mentored me in the Christian life focused
more on activities such as evangelism, mission and
service than on the Christian discipline of 'stillness'.
I wish I had been taught that Christian spirituality is
about developing a pure vision of God rather than a
full diary. I wish I'd been introduced to the mysterious
world 'beyond the veil' from day one, rather than
loaded with a set of devotional disciplines which
became a source of stress, failure and guilt.

I'm sure that the Christian leaders of the distant
past would have found our contemporary teaching on
prayer almost unintelligible, for they saw the whole
of life as spiritual. They believed that the Christian
pilgrim could only find true fulfilment by living their
whole life in the rich presence of Christ. Dr Christine
Sine's wonderful book *Sacred Rhythms* describes how

Celtic Christians looked to the rhythm of everyday life to give shape to their spirituality:

> Celtic Christians had prayers for every daily activity – from kindling the fire in the morning to milking the cow, and planting the crops in the fields. They gave these mundane events spiritual significance. Kindling the fire each day mirrored the coming of the light of Christ into their lives. Three days before planting time they sprinkled the seed with water in the name of the Father, Son and Holy Spirit. Seed was usually planted on a Friday, a symbol of Christ's death and burial and a reminder that Christ is the seed of the New World.

The Old Testament describes many different occasions when the whole nation's spirituality became focused on events lasting for a period of days or even weeks. There were the seasons of Pentecost, Shelters, Atonement, Passover, First fruits and Harvest, to name but a few. These were not single services or rituals, but focused periods of time given over to specific themes, disciplines of worship or sacrifice, or the telling of shared stories from their Jewish heritage.

If the stressed-out Christians of today are to survive the intense demands of our world, we need to develop longer seasons for our spiritual nourishment. We need times when we can focus on specific events in our lives or opportunities to develop and grow as people. I believe that contemporary Christianity has neglected our shared spiritual heritage and ignored the rich legacy of Christian mysticism which was integral to earlier Christian traditions. The devotional life has become a discipline, a process or a method, rather than a joyous experience which permeates the whole of life. I have known seasons of chastening and rebuke in my own life: times when I have been brought to my knees in humility and brokenness, times when I received a challenge to repent, times to make a new beginning and times to sort myself out with God.

There have also been seasons when my marriage, my fatherhood, my relationships with others and my growth as a human being have come under the spotlight of Christ's concern. There have been specific occasions when he has changed me through painful and chastening experiences.

Many Christians seem to want their spirituality dished out in palatable spoonfuls which can be absorbed in two minutes or less. When God wants to speak to me, however, I've found that he often takes weeks or even months to complete the process. He speaks as I live with a biblical theme, struggle with an aspect of personal transformation or test a new call over a prolonged length of time. It often takes months before I begin to grasp what God is really saying in my life.

I wish someone had explained all this to me all those years ago. I used to see my 'devotions' as a capsule of time outside normal life, a number of minutes specially allocated to spiritual discipline. Now, I see devotion as my availability to God in the cut and thrust of life. Spirituality is all about discovering what Christ is saying and doing in each season of my life. There have been seasons of special blessing, when the peace and power of Christ were especially real; times when prayer seemed natural and spontaneous, and when everyday life was imbued with a richer than usual sense of his presence. There have been seasons of special fruitfulness, when my ministry was used in a time of reaping; times when things seemed to be coming together and God's guidance was particularly real and clear.

When I first became a Christian no one told me about these seasons in the Christian life. I saw my devotional life as a daily allocation of time that remained the same, day in and day out, year in and year out. But now I recognize that my Christian spirituality is about identifying and getting the most from God's different activities in my life.

In the Dark Ages, St Aidan held out the light of Christ to a godless age. Through his influence much of England and Europe was affected by the Gospel. Yet Aidan was not based in a large city; his ministry was established on the island of Lindisfarne, known as Holy Island, off the Northumbrian coast. Lindisfarne is only a mile and a quarter from the shore. It's a tidal island and can only be approached when the tide is out. This gives a rhythm to its life. Aidan used to look out at a little boat at anchor to see whether the tide was coming in or going out. He built a discipline of spirituality on this daily flow of the tide. He taught his island community to receive the love of God as the tide came in, and then to pour it out in intercession, praise and loving service to others as the sea went out.

Aidan knew that too many lives become trivialized by too much action, and that each of us needs to be refreshed by the incoming tide of God's love. His view of devotion wasn't to do with ten minutes here or five minutes there, but was about seeing God in the daily flow of the sea. Everything was spiritual: the taking in and the giving out.

Each day, between the tide coming in and the tide going out, there was an hour when the tide was still. Aidan taught that when the balance between our receiving and our giving is right, we, like the still waters between tides, discover God's perfect peace.

Gradually, as more and more people visited Aidan and his praying community, he had to create another refuge away from Holy Island to restore the balance between the giving and the receiving in his own life. The tiny island where he did this was known as the 'desert in the ocean'. It was a place of great spiritual blessing but also a place where he fought the powers of darkness both within and without.

Aidan went there to be alone with God and to give priority to prayer. It was a wild and rugged place and his prayers were sometimes punctuated by the deafening roar of the sea. No one ever explained to me that there were other models of Christian spirituality than the traditional model of my evangelical culture. I find Aidan's understanding of spirituality in terms of incoming and outgoing tides particularly helpful.

I now see my life as the incoming flow of strength from God and the outgoing tide of my life poured out in service for Christ. But both the coming in and the giving out are spiritual, and both are equally important. My spirituality is about flowing with the tide of what God is doing, rather than asking him to fit in with some changeless formula of my own making.

Another of the early Christian mystics, St Anthony, described the experience of the stillness 'between tides'. He called it *hesychia*, the experience of entering into a state of stillness, tranquillity, or 'a silence of the heart'. *Hesychia* is attained when some upheaval in life destroys the old resources of intellect, and the new life is reached.

Gregory Palamas, a teacher of *hesychia*, described it as 'the standing still of the mind and of the world, forgetfulness of what is below, initiation into the knowledge of what is above, the putting aside of thoughts for what is better than they'. This, he said, 'is the ascent to the true contemplation and vision of God'.

I now believe, just as Aidan did, in the mystic rhythms of the spiritual life. My schedule is sometimes exhaustingly strenuous, but at other times more placid and reflective. Without the more reflective days I would have nothing to give in the more demanding times.

A devotional time lasting five minutes a day sets all the wrong parameters for me. I prefer to see my spiritual life in terms of tides or even seasons. My spirituality is less about reaching out for God in time-limited devotional slots, and more about discovering him in the holism of life's ebb and flow. Prayer has become less of an activity and more a state of being. God does not come to me in pre-packaged slots but in the breadth of the whole of my life and being. Christine Sine summed it up for me when she wrote

> We truly are people of rhythm and ritual, and amazingly, through the power of God's Spirit working in us, we hold within our grasp the possibility of shaping those rhythms and rituals in ways that intertwine our spiritual lives with everyday duties. We can take control of our lives and infuse them with rhythm that nourishes and maintains our faith and walk with God.

I am mortal; God is immortal. I am temporal; he is eternal. I am finite; he is infinite. I am human; he is God. Prayer takes me beyond the sphere of my knowing, beyond the material universe and into another dimension. Prayer is my approach to the One who is superior, pre-eminent, matchless and incomparable. Prayer is the moment when I touch the eternal, glimpse the holy, and am enfolded by perfect love. Prayer is moving beyond the confines of my own self-centredness to meet the One who created me and whose presence infuses me. For me, prayer has become life, and life prayer.

Union

Several years ago I was deeply concerned about a young peace campaigner called James Mawdsley who was languishing in a Burmese jail. His dad came on my radio programme and told the listeners how his son had sung a peace song and handed out twenty protest leaflets against the government in a public square in Burma.

James was arrested and tried by a one-man court, the official in question playing the competing roles of defence counsel, prosecution barrister and high court judge, all at the same time. He was sentenced to twenty years' imprisonment, with the prospect of many of them being spent in solitary confinement. With Premier Radio's help we managed to get hundreds of Christians to write to the Burmese embassy, and scores of listeners sent birthday cards to James in prison. Eventually, through a dramatic intervention by the then Foreign Secretary, the late Robin Cook, James was suddenly released and returned to London.

When he had recovered I interviewed him on my radio programme. I asked him what it felt like to be locked up in that stinking cell, with only a bowl of dirty rice each day and his own solitary company. He was not allowed mail or contact with his family or the outside world, and was even forbidden the use of a Bible.

'It must have been hell,' I said. 'No friends, no family and no future.' 'Quite the reverse,' he replied. 'It was like heaven. For when I realized that I literally had nothing, it was then that I realized that Jesus was enough.' With every other distraction removed, he had discovered the richness and all-pervasiveness of his union with Christ in a wretched prison cell. In the most dreadful of conditions he discovered that the wonder and richness of Christ was enough for him.

True union with Christ can sustain and nourish the human soul like nothing else. It is a joining of ourselves to God and a joining of God to ourselves. When the great Chinese teacher Watchman Nee was describing his experience of Christ, he took a very hot cup of tea, dropped a lump of sugar into it, and stirred it well. 'Now,' he said to the young man he was mentoring, 'try and take the sugar out of the tea.'

His young friend was exasperated. 'How can I? For the tea has become the sugar and the sugar has become the tea.'

'Exactly,' replied the great teacher. 'In the same way, I am in Christ and he is in me.'

Years after I first became a Christian this simple illustration helped me to grasp what it meant to follow Jesus. I discovered that my whole being is 'immersed in Christ, and he in me'. There is no aspect of who I am which his love does not reach or which his presence cannot infuse. This union with Christ is more intimate and more profound than any other human experience; it's a union greater than the intensity of human love or the passion of sexual intercourse. Some of my heroes in the faith have got into great trouble for comparing union with Christ to sexual ecstasy. Count von Zinzendorf, who founded the hundred-year prayer meeting and who is credited with starting the intercessory movement which led to the eighteenth-century revival, is a case in point. He was condemned and mocked by many of his Christian contemporaries for his use of sexual language to express the joy of union with Christ. But he was drawing on the poetic tradition rooted in the Song of Solomon and could find no greater expression for the ecstasy of being one with

Christ than sexual fulfilment. Zinzendorf described the adoration of the wounds of Jesus as an essential part of private and communal life.

I was never taught that this kind of intense experience of the presence of Christ was something that I should search for. No one explained that when I asked Christ into my life, I was actually asking to become united to him. I never understood that I was embarking on a life-long union which was so personal and intimate that it would touch every aspect of my being. This understanding of Christian experience is nothing new. The early church father Gregory wrote

> All that abides, abides in you alone, the movement of the Universe surges toward you – of all beings you are the goal. No matter where you may be, as long as your soul forms the sort of resting place in which God can dwell and linger, he will visit you.

True union with Christ is not something that I have to work at, but something I receive – a grace that comes as part of the Christian experience. Union with Christ is the most wonderful experience of life itself. Madame Guyon, writing at the end of the seventeenth century, wrote a powerful book on spirituality called *Experiencing the Depths of Jesus Christ*. It's a book which has enriched the lives of countless Christians down the centuries. She wrote

> Dear child of God, all your concepts of what God is really like amount to nothing. Do not try to imagine what God is like. Instead, simply believe in his presence. Never try to imagine what God will do. There is no way God will ever fit into your concepts. What then shall you do? Seek to behold Jesus Christ by looking to him in your inmost being, in your spirit.

It is this abiding union with Christ, of which Madame Guyon writes, which has carried me through some of the hardest times of my life. Sometimes I have had no evidence that he was there, but have clung on to the promise of this fusion of my life with his.

As time has passed, my sense of union with Christ has grown more real. Even now, forty years after I first came to know him, I am discovering yet more of its richness and reality. Why didn't anyone tell me? Why didn't anyone let me into the mystery described by Dame Julian of Norwich in her classic book *Revelations of Divine Love*

> When our Lord gives us the grace of revealing himself to our soul, we have what we desire. At that time we are not interested in praying for anything else, because all our attention is fixed on contemplating him. This is a very exalted type of prayer that cannot, in my opinion, be described, because the origin of our prayer has been united to the sight and the vision of the One to whom we pray; wondering, enjoying, venerating, fearing him with such sweetness and delight that for the duration we can only pray in the way that he inspires us.

Passion

A few months ago I stood on the Mount of Olives and looked down over Jerusalem. I remembered the time when Jesus looked over that same city and wept:

> O Jerusalem, Jerusalem, you who kill the prophets and stone those sent to you, how often I have longed to gather your children together, as a hen gathers her chicks under her wings, but you were not willing (Mt. 23:37).

Jesus had an aching burden for the people of that great city. He knew their needs and wanted to embrace them with his love. These were no empty sentiments, but the expression of One who lived entirely for others. Jesus loved the world with a depth of compassion that we can't begin to understand. My view of intercession has gradually changed. I used to think of it as a kind of shopping list of need, for me, my loved ones and the world. But now I see it less as words and more as an expression of my deepest feelings. I'm with Paul when he wrote

> We do not know what we ought to pray for, but the Spirit himself intercedes for us with groans that words cannot express. And he who searches our hearts knows the mind of the Spirit, because the Spirit intercedes for the saints in accordance with God's will (Rom. 8:26-27).

I don't believe he wants me to gabble a list of things I want him to do. He knows the list before I arrive, anyway. No, he wants to read my heart. He wants to see if I care, to know that I feel the burden, and to recognize that I am emotionally engaged with what I'm asking him to do. J. Oswald Sanders, the great teacher on the spiritual life, taught that 'all true praying comes from the Spirit's activity in our souls'.

Both Paul and Jude teach that effective prayer is 'praying in the Spirit'. This phrase means that we pray along the same lines, about the same things, and in the same way as the Holy Spirit. True prayer rises in the spirit of the Christian from the Spirit who dwells in us.

When I pray for others, I'm less worried about getting the words in the right order and much more concerned to feel the needs I'm expressing. I can only pray effectively if my concern is genuine. For too long I prayed as I had been taught – from the head and not from the heart. I believe that true intercession transcends words. As I prepare to intercede for the world, I try to move from seeing the suffering around me to feeling it. When I weep with those who weep, I really intercede. Prayer for others is not what I thought it was when I first became a Christian. It's not a list of names and situations to be recited like a child's requests whispered into the ear of Father Christmas. It's a cry from the heart to a loving Father who moves in ways beyond my understanding. I am convinced that true prayer is empowered by raw emotion.

One of the strangest and most enthusiastic tour guides I ever worked with helped me to lead a party around the seven churches of Asia. She was always passionate about her subject, and although not a Christian, she shed a tear or two whenever our group gathered for prayer. She explained that very few groups ever got to visit Laodicea, because the general feeling in the tourist industry was that there 'wasn't enough to see there'.

She evidently felt differently, for she ordered our driver to take the coach through a moonscape of rugged rocky countryside and then told him to stop, seemingly in the middle of nowhere.

When we disembarked, she led us down a rough track until we began to see ruined walls, ancient pillars and faded mosaics that were only freshly uncovered by the archaeologist's trowel.

We sat by the remains of an amphitheatre and gazed at the spectacular view. High on the hill to our right was the distant lime-covered cliff where stood the temple and religious ruins of Hieropolis. To our left, far beneath us, was a main road and a bustling conurbation.

With breathless enthusiasm she pointed to the steaming springs by the temple. 'When the water began to descend,' she explained, 'it was hot and steaming, bubbling straight from the hot springs beneath the earth. By the time it had descended the mountain it was cold. But here, at Laodicea, halfway down, it was lukewarm and disgusting.' I opened my Bible and read out loud, 'I know your deeds, that you are neither cold nor hot. I wish you were either one or the other! So, because you are lukewarm – neither hot nor cold – I am about to spit you out of my mouth' (Rev. 3:15-16).

Sometimes when I hear prayers in church they are recited like a monotonous drone of requests and I really wonder if God is listening. These words are neither hot nor cold, and the emotions of the one who is leading are evidently not engaged. Christian author Dr Gary Smalley, writing in *The DNA of Relationships*, observed

> Most of us do not understand the role that emotions are supposed to play in who we are. We do not appreciate how God designed us to function as fully emotional beings. Your brain is the processor, the decision-maker. But without the good data supplied by your emotions, the processor has little to work with. And of what use is a processor without good data? God designed you to work best when your mind and your soul work together. You make the best decisions when you use your feelings to inform your brain. To get the best result, you need both your emotions and your intellect.

Prayer for others is powerless without the passion of our emotions to drive it forward. It's pointless unless imbued with the kind of faith which can move mountains. Let our praying be either hot or cold, but God save it from being lukewarm.

I don't know how intercession works, but I know that it does. The ability of the Lord to hear and to respond to each of us is beyond my understanding. I know that his capacity for this is vast, all-embracing and yet intensely personal.

Someone once told me of a proud mother who was describing her son's achievements at school to her minister. She took out the huge school photograph and carefully unrolled it. The picture depicted hundreds of microscopic faces, but instantly she pointed to one face and declared, 'There he is!' Among the hundreds of children pictured she knew immediately which was her son.

I know that God doesn't forget me, that my name is engraved on the palm of his hand, and that even among so many I am special to him. When I enter the holy place I am recognized, I am known, I am understood. In fact, the burdens of my heart are heard and known long before I even enter.

Once, when I was on holiday on the beautiful Greek island of Lesbos, I walked into an ancient monastery, where Ignatius is buried. I ambled down the long, shady cloister and gazed in wonder at the beautiful scrolls inscribed by his followers; some of these faded parchments were over fifteen hundred years old. As I stood beside the tomb of this early church leader I sensed the timelessness of God's kingdom and the eternal perspective of my heavenly Father. In an instant I saw my tiny life within the broad reach of God's purposes and my life as but a fragment in his vast design. I was overwhelmed by God's greatness and my own insignificance.

But then, at that moment, I looked beside the tomb and saw the figure of a tiny dead sparrow. Immediately I felt confronted by the words of Jesus: 'Are not five sparrows sold for two pennies? Yet not one of them is forgotten by God. ... Don't be afraid; you are worth more than many sparrows' (Lk. 12:6-7). That tiny lifeless body conveyed God's enormous love for me. I saw that his care for every part of what he has made continues undimmed across the centuries. My Lord cares about sparrows, and he also cares about me. I am not forgotten.

There is no aspect of my life outside his knowledge; there is nothing he doesn't understand and no insecurity of which he's unaware. As I looked at the sparrow I recognized again that every breath is a gift of God and that my very life is mysteriously bound up with him. He remembers me. It's his amazing love and care which give me confidence when I enter the holy place. I can bring my prayers and petitions straight to the Lord Jesus, who is constantly praying for me. I need no priest, no intermediary, no religious 'middle-man'.

> This is the confidence we have in approaching God: that if we ask anything according to his will, he hears us. And if we know that he hears us – whatever we ask – we know that we have what we asked of him (1 Jn. 5:14-15).

Relationship

God made us for relationship, and our ability to have and develop relationships is part of what makes us unique as human beings.

When I first became a Christian, no one explained to me that I could actually meet Christ in other people. I recognized, of course, that Christian fellowship was good, but I always saw it as best expressed in the singing of hymns, the saying of prayers or the breaking of bread together. I never understood that true Christian fellowship is an intensely spiritual experience.

Since those early days I've become more and more aware of Christ in others. In fact, some of my most profound experiences of Jesus have been in discovering him through relationship with others. I've met him in the precious silences between friends as well as in words, hugs and laughter. Christians recognize that at the cornerstone of the universe there is a relationship between Father, Son and Holy Spirit. It's a relationship of perfect love, perfect unity and yet separate identity. Relationship is at the very heart of Christianity. It's a relationship which existed before the planet and one which will outlast history. It's the true model for all good human relationships. Christians cannot deny the importance of rich relationship without denying the very character of God himself. We get an insight into the quality of relationship between Jesus and his heavenly Father in John 17:

> Father, the time has come. Glorify your Son, that your Son may glorify you. For you granted him authority over all people that he might give eternal life to all those you have given him. ... All I have is yours, and all you have is mine (Jn. 17: 1-2,10).

It's a prayer full of affirmation. It's about trust – for Jesus recognized that his authority flowed from the Father (Jn. 17:1-2) – but that trust involved complete obedience. Most beautiful of all, the prayer demonstrates that Father and Son share a relationship of intimacy.

There are no masks and there's no pretending, for they know each other and love each other completely (v. 3). Little wonder, then, that it's not a short-lived or transient relationship but eternal. It's a relationship of intimate sharing and complete understanding (v. 10) and it lasts for ever.

Sometimes shafts of light break through the Bible text to show us how we should live our lives. These verses have helped me to see that relationships are important to God and that Christ is very present in the richness they bring. Sometimes we might also meet him when we meet a complete stranger. Hebrews 13:2 says, 'Do not forget to entertain strangers, for by so doing some people have entertained angels without knowing it.' One of the prayers of the Celtic church emphasizes the truth of this:

> We saw a stranger yesterday,
> We put food in the eating place,
> Drink in the drinking place,
> Music in the listening place,
> And with the sacred name of the triune God
> He blessed us and our house,
> Our cattle and our dear ones.
> As the lark says in her song:
> Often, often, often
> Goes the Christ in the stranger's guise.

We were created not to live lonely isolated lives, but to meet each other in the intimacy of beautiful lasting relationships. These relationships are what make each day special, for they reflect our value to God and to each other.

Fearing that his days were numbered after a major heart attack, Dr Gary Smalley observed

> I realized anew that the most important thing in my life is relationships – not only with my family and friends

and the people I meet all over the world, but with the God who walks with me even 'through the dark valley of death.' The rest is just details.

Our sense of belonging to one another is at the core of what it means to be human. The depth of our relationships is a sign that God is present. True fellowship is not, as many church newsletters advertise it, 'a cup of tea and a biscuit'.

Fellowship occurs when we discover each other, and in that discovery find the presence of Christ. It's not so much about unity as about union; about relating to each other at a level which exemplifies what it means to belong to Christ.

M. Scott Peck defined the quality of the kind of relationship I'm thinking of when he wrote in *The Different Drum* of the uniqueness of the Christian community

> Community is a safe place precisely because no one is attempting to heal or convert you, to fix you, to change you. Instead, the members accept you as you are. You are free to be you. And being so free, you are free to discard defences, masks, disguises; free to seek your own psychological and spiritual health; free to become your whole and holy self.

Christian relationships differ from those of the world because of our understanding of the uniqueness of personhood and the sanctity of each human individual. In *Whatever Happened to the Human Race?* Francis Schaeffer wrote

> Each man, woman and child is of great value, not for some ulterior motive such as self gratification, or wealth,

or power, or as a sex object or for the good of society, but because of his or her origin. God has created every human being 'in his own image'.

It's little wonder, then, that where we share fellowship he is there. I first studied the first epistle of John when I was at Bible College at the age of 19. I've never forgotten the challenging words, 'Whoever does not love does not know God, because God is love.' (1 Jn. 4:8). I remember that all those years ago, these words didn't seem to fit my rather orthodox evangelical Gospel.

I wish that someone had told me, all those years ago, that this verse is true. For love changes people. I've seen it change others, and I've known it change me. God is the source of creative and positive change in us through rich relationships because he *is* love. When we love others by caring, by serving and by self-giving, we discover that God is present. As we offer sacrificial love we give him space to come. When we love for no other motive than to celebrate the One who is Love, his presence floods our lives.

I've come to see that relationship is at the centre of my spirituality. The relationships I share with others are often opportunities for God to speak, and I am now aware that even when I meet a stranger, I may be welcoming Jesus himself.

No one told me this, and I could so easily have missed this precious gift along the way.

4

What they didn't tell me about the church

Pilgrim people

I think a lot of pain in my life would have been avoided if someone had taken me aside and helped me to come to terms with the church. As it was, no one helped me to get to grips with a biblical understanding of what it really is.

I was brought up in the life of the church, I endured four years of liberal theological education and I struggled for over eight years with the institutional paralysis of local church ministry. I have spent hours of my time with young Christians who have been disillusioned and sometimes even broken by what they have seen in the 'established' churches.

I have a great love for the denomination in which I was reared, an awesome regard for its history and a heartfelt desire to see it renewed. I have often been battered and bruised by that same institution, and have sometimes felt that I didn't belong, or even that it wasn't for me.

More than ten years ago I made some pretty tough decisions. I looked back across the years in which I had fought choirmasters about church music, finance officers about the use of funds and institutional leaders about what I saw as major errors in national policy, and decided that I didn't want to invest my time in that kind of conflict any more.

I arrived at the rather startling and painful conclusion that time is short, the task urgent, and that I should invest my remaining energy in planting new things rather than in attempting to root up the old. I decided that for my own sanity and emotional well-being I needed to move away from those old institutional battles.

Looking back, I can see that many of the biggest conflicts of my early ministry led to nothing but an overwhelming sense of frustration. I had, quite simply, been there and done that and I'd had enough of it. Some would say that I opted out, walked away or evaded my responsibilities, but I don't regret it. I believe that the institutional church has developed a strange ability to engage countless people in a struggle for power and influence. It's a kind of conflict which saps them of creative energy and distracts them from the vital work of mission. These battles leave many dynamic Christian leaders drained of the kind of strength and vision which should be used to reach the world for Christ.

I wish someone had warned me in my early days as a minister against fighting all those time-consuming battles. I wish they had warned me against becoming locked in conflicts with others who, though headed in the wrong direction, are trying to do their best for God. I wish someone had shown me that I could waste so much time on institutional Christianity that I could miss out on the greater joy of 'being church'. No one taught me that the real fun of Christian ministry is about seeing young people find Christ, discover their God-given gifts and move out into dynamic Christian service in the world. Battles with the institution are a very poor alternative.

I wish someone had encouraged me to focus on things that God is using and blessing, instead of trying to breathe fresh life and energy into the stuff that is long past its sell-by date.

There are many things in the life of the denominational churches which have no Kingdom value: Structures built on the concepts of men rather than the will of God: Hallowed traditions which, sadly, do little but exclude others from the Kingdom. Such things may have served a distant age, but in a secularized and disinterested society they need to be quietly disposed of. The yawning gap between the culture of the institutional church and the culture of the world seems to grow every year. Time is short, and I want to invest my days in the vision of the young pioneers who are dreaming a new dream and taking Christian mission onto the front line. I don't want to waste my time in political in-fighting, or in 'fiddling while Rome burns'.

I shudder to think that so many have spent so long fighting pitched battles in deadlocked committees which did nothing to heal a broken world. In my early years I was drawn into the work of sustaining religious institutions rather than working on the real building, the living temple of the people of God. The true church of Christ is never a people stuck in the past but a people on the move, a pilgrim people journeying with God. I want to be part of this dynamic movement and to make my contribution to this community which is constantly seeking God's way ahead.

The New Testament theology of church had nothing to do with preserving buildings, traditions or religious institutions. The word which Paul and the other New Testament writers used for 'church' was *ekklesia*. It's a word that survives in our language today – in our word 'ecclesiastical'. There was nothing stuffy or traditional about the word when it was first coined. *Ekklesia* goes back to two words in Hebrew: *edah*, which was used for any important meeting of the nation, and *qahal*, which meant to summon or to call together. It was an action word, implying movement and impending change for a community forever travelling from the old to the new. It was a word strongly associated with the Exodus, Israel's miraculous escape from Egypt, and God's providential care for them during their long years on the journey to the Promised Land. Just as he had called the people of Israel to a journey of faith, he calls us to move ever forward to a new adventure with him.

In Acts we read how Stephen refers to the Israelites on Mount Sinai as 'the church in the wilderness'. The scholar Cerfaux argues that this passage shows the origin of the Christian usage of the word 'church'. The word *ekklesia*, therefore, showed that Christians were the people who had been 'called out' to become the New Israel. They belonged to a new community, and Jesus was the new Moses who was gathering his people in preparation for the last days. The church was a pilgrim people making its journey to God's Promised Land.

In Ephesians 2, Paul reminded the Gentile community about how much Christ had done for them. They had been called out of their old life of sin and shame, guilt and failure, separation from God and the hopelessness of the Law. They had been called to a new life, a new relationship with God, a new Kingdom, and a daily adventure of faith. They were part of a community which was travelling from the old to the new.

> ... at that time you were separate from Christ, excluded from citizenship in Israel and foreigners to the covenants of the promise, without hope and without God in the

world. But now in Christ Jesus you who once were far away have been brought near through the blood of Christ (Eph. 2:12-13).

I wish someone had given me permission to stop wasting time on things which have no eternal value, and had helped me to avoid spending my time on preserving traditions which are best buried. I wish someone had invited me to invest my energies in the pilgrim people, the community of those who make up the living church. They are the ones travelling on into the unknown, the people committed to the real adventures of God's Kingdom. The church of God is a gathering of people who are making this journey together. It's a physical journey of people who accompany each other along the way. It's a spiritual journey of those on the road from darkness to light. It's a timeless journey from here to eternity. It's a journey of those willing to respond to the changing demands of the world around them. It's a journey with the people who are on the move for God and who are constantly responding to his leading as they seek the way ahead.

Mentors

I think that many of my struggles as a Christian would have been lessened if, when I first became a believer, someone had been put on my case to disciple and mentor me.

I have the vaguest memories of something called a church membership class, which gave me a basic understanding of what being a Christian was all about. But I headed off down the road of discipleship with no one specifically appointed to guide me or to make sure

I was going in the right direction. My formation as a Christian was very much a do-it-yourself affair, and as a result I didn't learn some basic lessons until I had travelled several years down the road of discipleship.

Looking back, I can see how much I would have gained if I had been properly apprenticed in the Christian life. I had lived the life of a committed Christian for over fifteen years before I discovered the rich possibilities of such a relationship.

I was a minister in a London suburb when a bizarre sequence of events brought me into contact with Clive, an evangelical pastor in the same area. The local newspaper pitted us against each other in an article when the controversial film *Life of Brian* was first screened. We met shortly afterwards, and prayed together that God would use this unfortunate incident for something good.

Ever since, for over twenty years, we have met regularly for prayer and reflection. Clive's input to my life at these meetings has been incalculable, and his teaching from the Scriptures has built a long-term mentoring relationship in my life. Without it, my life as a Christian would have been considerably poorer.

I'm convinced that all Christians should see themselves as apprentices in the spiritual life and should seek guidance from those who have travelled further along the journey than they have. We all need spiritual directors who can navigate our hungry souls towards the feast of good things which God has prepared for us.

St Aidan, the founder of the ancient Lindisfarne community, recognized that it isn't easy for any of us to develop a life of prayer and contemplation, so he set up a system of mentoring to encourage his followers to learn these disciplines.

Each of the Lindisfarne brothers whom he personally mentored adopted an *anamchara* – a cell-mate. This new member of the community had to learn by rote 150 psalms, one of the Gospels and the spiritual songs which were taught him by the senior brother. In turn the younger member would take on his own *anamchara* and so pass on the spiritual disciplines from one generation to another.

I'm encouraged that spiritual mentoring in the contemporary church is becoming much more popular again. Many committed Christians are discovering that their lives are greatly enriched when they find a spiritual director to help them in their personal journey of prayer and devotion. A spiritual director can help us to make sense of everyday life and to spot God's activity in the mundane. Through regular contact with such a person, we can get some perspective on our lives and gain great benefit from their maturity and experience.

Every Christian should be encouraged to find a spiritual director, someone to help them assess their development in the Christian life, to point out areas of weakness and to support initiatives for change and growth. Above all, a spiritual director should provide accountability and give the kind of wise guidance which leads to spiritual maturity.

My prayer partner has been an invaluable source of strength to me over the last twenty years. There have been times when we have laughed uncontrollably and times when we have wept together. We have shared the deep hurts of life and the great joys of God's blessing, and it has been enormously enriching.

After so many years he can read me accurately, and his care for my soul is something which, though sometimes uncomfortable, is always helpful. I wish I had recognized the importance of this in my early days. Why didn't anyone tell me that this is how the church is supposed to work? I believe that the *anamchara* relationship is integral to the church's health and renewal.

The Temple

Several years ago I stayed on holiday in a seventeenth-century villa in the mountains of Provence in southern France. The house was a tall, rambling structure built into the mountainside and miles from anywhere. As I drove up the rough mountain track towards the house I saw a large gap in the front wall, which revealed a huge stone: a cornerstone. The whole building was constructed around it. I don't know why the builders chose to leave the stone exposed, but it was a lovely reminder that the whole house was built around something completely immovable and secure. The church is built on an unshakeable cornerstone, which is Jesus Christ. All who are committed to him are the stones of the building. It is as the stones are built together that the Temple of God takes shape.

> Welcome to the living stone, the source of life. The workmen took one look and threw it out; God set it in the place of honour. Present yourselves as building stones for the construction of a sanctuary vibrant with life, in which you'll serve as holy priests offering Christ-approved lives up to God (1 Pet. 2:4-5, The Message).

Paul told the Ephesians that they should not feel like strangers in the holy place, for they themselves were God's building – the temple. Each one had a special place to fill, and a responsibility to be joined together with the rest of God's building.

God is building a home. He's using us all – irrespective of how we got here – in what he is building. He used the apostles and prophets for the foundation. Now he's using you, fitting you in brick by brick, stone by stone, with Christ Jesus as the cornerstone that holds all the parts together. We see it taking shape day after day – a holy temple built by God, all of us built into it, a temple in which God is quite at home (Eph. 2:19-22, The Message).

With the passage of time this concept of the 'living temple' has become more and more important to me. Jesus is the cornerstone, the apostles and prophets are the foundation, and as we take our place within it, the walls grow higher and the living temple becomes more beautiful.

The interconnectedness of the structure is what makes the whole thing stand. It's a togetherness which flows from the cornerstone to the foundations, and from the foundations to the growing walls. The living temple takes shape because it's connected and joined. No one explained that I needed to be closely connected to what had gone before. No one helped me to find my place in the living temple. No one explained that I needed older and wiser Christians to help to knock my edges off and to show me how to become part of God's mysterious temple, the spiritual entity which stretches from ancient history towards the clouds of eternity.

This holy temple is made up of people who live in the real world, each of whom is a powerful witness to the living God. This temple is never a place, but always a people, never a sacred building but always a believing assembly. The church is we who pray, not where we pray. I wish someone had introduced me to the mysterious privilege of belonging to this holy temple. I wish I'd understood that each brick and stone is valuable, integral and beautiful, and how wonderful it is to be joined and connected to Christians everywhere in this mysterious building, a temple that's still under construction.

Ministry

In the early days of my Christian life I was drawn into becoming the servant of an institution rather than a member of the Body of Christ. Looking back, I can see that was a depressing experience which didn't do me a lot of good. No one warned me that I could waste so much time on something that wasn't what it claimed to be. At that time my growth into Christian maturity was closely associated with an ever-increasing commitment to the institution, but later I came to realize that these two things were largely incompatible.

I grew up in a church which has evolved into a complex machine. Nationwide there is a labyrinth of committees, officers and hierarchies. This multi-layered organization is often locked in a kind of power play between its different departments. It engages large numbers of people in the processes of its management. For some time I was trapped in its complex systems.

As a young Christian I recognized that the institution demanded the time of large numbers of people to service its needs. I was persuaded that I could help it to function better by giving input to its endless committees, by supporting its numerous officers and by taking my turn in fulfilling its multifarious roles. I was quickly drawn into this strange world of denominationalism.

Even now, many young Christians find themselves invited to attend committees, to go through induction courses, to gain church-recognized qualifications, to be sent as representatives to conferences, to read set books, to take on major organizational responsibilities and show up for visiting VIPs. When they talk with excitement about the 'opportunities' they've been given I want to ask, 'But is it right?'

Over the last few years I've been privileged to help a group of young preachers who are being trained so that the church can accredit them. As I have become involved in this process, I have seen clearly the huge disconnection between the needs of this group and the needs of the organization which they wish to serve.

The systems developed to test their call are based on what the institution needs rather than on what they need. When they began the preaching course they were the most exciting and visionary group of people that it's been my privilege to support for some years. But I have watched in horror as a creeping disillusion has overcome them. The systems have not worked. There's been no attempt to match their training to their previous educational experience. They've received critical letters from people three times their age, which were largely unwarranted. Their evangelical faith has been dubbed 'naive' and their preaching style 'insensitive'. They have sat in committees, hearing complaints about their contribution to the preaching ministry from people whose own ministry leaves much to be desired.

The inability of the inflexible organization to meet their needs has left me despondent and frustrated. The enormous gifts which this group were bringing to the church have been dismissed and publicly rejected. There is a huge discrepancy between the needs of the institution and the needs of those who long to serve the Body of Christ.

In this training process there seemed no acknowledgement that these people were God's gift to the church, that they were testing God's call rather than getting a denominational certificate, or that their ministry was about supporting the Body of Christ rather than filling empty pulpits.

There is a dearth of biblical understanding about the Body of Christ in the denominational churches. We appoint people to jobs instead of discovering their God-given role in the Body. We push them into doing things that are not part of their calling or for which they are not equipped. We misuse the resources which God has given to the church. We call people to serve the processes of a dead institution rather than the commission of a living God.

No one sat down with me and helped me to identify the gifts God had given me. No one mentored me in how my gifts could best be used in his service. No one guided me as to where I should invest my time in Christian service so that it might have the greatest effect. No one sought to listen to God's will for my life or gave me a steer concerning how God might want to use a person like me.

There are some great resources around today which can help each of us to identify our gifts and to understand what kind of people we are. Over the last five years I've been through three different questionnaire programmes, each of which was supported by Christian leaders who had a healthy balance of perception and spiritual maturity. I have felt greatly affirmed that all three 'strength-finder' programmes came back with the same set of answers. They identified that my strongest gifts are as a forward thinker, advanced planner and visionary leader, but I had reached fifty years of age before I recognized these gifts within me or felt affirmed in using them. I can only pray that the young Christians of the rising generation won't have to wait so long.

The Body

I wish that when I first became a Christian someone had encouraged me to grapple with the biblical teaching about the Body of Christ. If I had understood it, I think I would have taken off this straitjacket of institutional Christianity much sooner and discovered what it meant to be a fully functioning part of the Body of Christ. If I'd really understood what it meant to belong to the Body of Christ, I think I would have moved from paralysis to mobility in my ministry more quickly. I think I would have become part of God's coordinated team much sooner.

The Bible teaches that every part of the Body of Christ, be it a struggling local congregation or a national church institution, must be submitted to the Head and must live under the Lordship of Jesus Christ. Every part must be responsive to his will and strive to fulfil his agenda. You may be able to survive without an arm or a leg, a finger or an appendix, but you'd not survive long without a head! The head coordinates and controls the various parts of the body and empowers them to fulfil their different functions.

The Body of Christ works well when it lives under the authority of the Head. Creeping institutionalism grows when there is a lack of submission to the Head. When this happens, the members of the Body don't receive the right signals, don't run in coordination with each other, and aren't properly submitted to the will of him to whom the Body belongs. In this kind of situation Christ does not have the supremacy. Paul reminds us of how things should be:

> He is before all things, and in him all things hold together. And he is the head of the body, the church; he

is the beginning and the firstborn from among the dead,
so that in everything he might have the supremacy (Col.
1:17-18).

Sadly, some parts of the Body of Christ have been
paralysed by structures which have sought to control,
restrict and manage them. If the Body is to function
properly, God's people need to be released for mission.
There is no argument between two legs as to which
one should step out first, or between four fingers as to
which one will point the way. Paul wrote

The body is a unit, though it is made up of many parts;
and though all its parts are many, they form one body (1
Cor. 12:12).

No one in my early days as a Christian encouraged
me to question those hierarchical models of church life
which paralyse individual action and local initiative.
No one helped me to understand that the local church
should always be at the cutting edge and free to respond
to the changing scene. No one taught me that the
denominations need to turn away from servicing their
own needs in order to discover how best to empower
the local people for mission. They need to put their
energy into releasing people in their gifts rather than
attempting to keep them in line. I don't believe that the
church can move forward by consensus, by committee
or by systems of government which are looking for a
safe majority. It will advance by initiative, by risk, and
by obedience to the great commission. Christ rules the
Body. He knows the way ahead. Every aspect of the
church's life must be submitted to his authority.

And God placed all things under his feet and appointed
him to be head over everything for the church, which is

his body, the fullness of him who fills everything in every way (Eph. 1:22-23).

Human paralysis comes when parts of the body fail to function. Damage to the spinal cord can result in paralysed legs. A broken arm can restrict the movement of the hand. Blind eyes or deaf ears slow down the body's effectiveness. Those parts in the life of the church which aren't functioning need major surgery if the Body of Christ is to move in coordinated response towards Kingdom goals.

Each member of the Body needs to play their part and to fulfil their calling. Each believer must be appointed and supported in fulfilling the role in the Body which is theirs and theirs alone.

> Just as each of us has one body with many members, and these members do not all have the same function, so in Christ we who are many form one body, and each member belongs to all the others. We have different gifts, according to the grace given us (Rom. 12:4-6).

There's nothing institutional about the way this Body works, because it's joined by deep bonds of compassion and care. Paul's metaphor makes the point. When the tooth aches, the whole body suffers. When the finger is cut, the body's defences are marshalled for healing. When the heart aches, the eyes shed tears. The people of Christ share a deep sense of interconnectedness which the world can never understand.

The Body of Christ doesn't work properly without this rich sense of belonging. If this were missing, it would live without feeling, without sensitivity and without caring: a body paralysed.

> If one part suffers, every part suffers with it; if one part is honoured, every part rejoices with it (1 Cor. 12:26).

If we really are the Body of Christ, we must discover the rich sense of belonging that he created us for. No part of the Body has any greater worth than another, 'On the contrary,' Paul writes, 'those parts of the body that seem to be weaker are indispensable ...' (1 Cor. 12:22).

There is much for the people of God to do, for together we represent the life of Jesus here on earth. He has a massive agenda to complete, and we are the people through whom he wants to work. We must take off the institutional straitjacket and free ourselves of this organizational paralysis. We must become the Body of Christ!

I wish that someone had told me what it's really like to be the Body of Christ: all connected; all functioning; all healthy; all coordinated; all released; all working together. This Body exists today, and it runs within and outside the institutional churches. It's where the life is, where the growth is, where the vision is, where the risk is, and where the gifts of God's people are being used properly. The Body is not to be found in the cold rule books of institutional Christianity, but where there is love, laughter and the joyful discovery of our God-given gifts.

Leadership

My journey towards Christian leadership began in the study of the principal of Cliff College when I was just 19 years old. The Rev Howard Belben smiled a warm smile and informed me that I was soon to lead a six-man team for a six-week mission. We were to live by faith and to serve the crowds of holidaymakers in Blackpool. I would be responsible for the vision, organization and discipline of the team of young men in my care. I nearly fell off my chair! I'd never seen myself as a leader, but evidently he had seen that gift within me. That six-week adventure was one of the most formative experiences of my life. I will never forget it, nor the lessons which I learnt through it. It was, for me, one of those experiences which charted the direction of everything which followed.

Apart from that, however, in my early years as a Christian leader no one explained what Christian leadership was about. In four years of theological training for ministry I can't recall a single lecture on the subject. There continues to be a kind of assumption in many areas of ministerial training that the overall aim is to produce middle managers rather than dynamic leaders with a real vision for the future.

My early years in Christian leadership were developed in the 'one-man band' school of ministry. The one-man band, of course, is typically a musician whose skill is legendary but whose music is appalling. Few others can match his ability, but the end result is excruciating. He carries a bass drum on his back and has cymbals between his knees. There's a mouth organ suspended from his head and a trombone in his hand. From time to time, in perfect rhythm, he beats the bass drum with drumsticks strapped to his elbows. He is a spectacle to watch, but agonizing to listen to.

I was very much a one-man band in my early life as a Christian leader. It's a model of ministry which is still popular in many contemporary churches, whether the leader be called vicar, minister, priest, elder or deacon. Whatever the title, the role is much the same. She or he is the 'one-man band', trying to do six things at once and doing none of them particularly well. This kind of ministry is a discordant cacophony, and much energy is expended to little lasting effect. Much of my early ministry was like this, and no one explained to me that there was a better, God-ordained way.

The church has come to rely on 'one-man bands' to do much of its work. It places layers of responsibility on shoulders not strong enough to carry them. The one-man band struggles from day to day trying to do the work of administrator, evangelist, pastor, caretaker, worship leader, diplomat, civil servant, preacher and prophet. Meanwhile, the members of the congregation are spectators rather than participants. Trying to live this model of leadership nearly broke me. As I travel the country today, I can see that it's still breaking many others.

This was not the early church model of Christian leadership. There is no biblical evidence to support the idea that the work of the church is to be done by paid professionals who are 'good at everything'. The role of the leader in the New Testament was not to do the work himself, but to envision, equip and empower others to join him in the doing of it. The early church taught that all the members are the *laos* – the people – who have been called out of society to serve God and others. There was no suggestion of a hierarchy or different levels of status, because all the believers were part of the church's mission and they all belonged to the people of God.

Peter made it clear that everyone is a member of the team when he wrote

> But you are a chosen people, a royal priesthood, a holy nation, a people belonging to God, that you may declare the praises of him who called you out of darkness into his wonderful light. Once you were not a people, but now you are the people of God ... (1 Pet. 2:9-10).

George Newlands, in *The Church of God*, noted

> ... the purpose of the whole Christian community is
> 'diaconia', service, and in this sense there is a priesthood
> of all believers. This service is entirely dependent on
> Christ, and on his continuing ministry through the Holy
> Spirit.

Over the years I've turned away from the one-man
band model. I'm convinced that the emerging church
does not need more multi-skilled people to do its work
alone. I'm committed to changing the expectations of
local churches which are still looking for such a person.
The key to a healthy and growing church is not a
'superstar' leader but a team of local Christians who
are all empowered to play their part in that church's
life. The early church was not a parade of one-man
bands. The letters of leaders like Peter and Paul were
letters of encouragement and inspiration to local people
to fulfil their own ministry and to develop their own
priestly role.

> You also, like living stones, are being built into a spiritual
> house to be a holy priesthood, offering spiritual sacrifices
> acceptable to God through Jesus Christ (1 Pet. 2:5).

The biblical concept of church leadership is not based
on the concept of the 'star performer', but rather on
the leader who enables each of the people of God to
fulfil their calling. Leadership is not about status in the
hierarchy, but about servanthood in the Body.

> There are different kinds of gifts, but the same Spirit.
> There are different kinds of service, but the same Lord.
> There are different kinds of working, but the same God
> works all of them in all men. Now to each one the

manifestation of the Spirit is given for the common good
(1 Cor. 12:4-7).

John P. Kotter of Harvard Business School, in his book
The Leadership Factor, makes a clear distinction between
leadership and management. Leadership has vision,
communicates it, and has the ability to get people to
follow. Such leaders can recruit and motivate people
to work to the vision by inspiring and directing them.
This is different from the management function which
ensures an efficient and effective use of resources.
Managers have an ability to organize and administrate
and are essential, but they represent something different
from leadership.

For generations, our theological colleges have been
turning out one-man bands: high achievers and polished
performers who can preach, administrate, manage and
counsel. In every role they perform, they parade their
own abilities but do not develop the gifts of others.
We need instead leaders who aren't one-man bands
but are conductors of orchestras, who prefer to create
beautiful symphonies. They hear new harmonies and
communicate the wonder of the music to those who've
never heard it. They don't want to perform the music
on their own, but to share the joy of creativity with all
the other players.

This kind of visionary leader can draw together
a mighty orchestra, with each player committed to
their task. They are facilitators, not performers, whose
greatest thrill is to see the orchestra playing in perfect
harmony. When this is accomplished, they step back
into the shadows, knowing that the vision is fulfilled,
the dream has come true. Christian leaders must be
encouraged to develop personal vision and taught
how to impart this vision to others. In four years of

theological education I never heard anything about vision or empowerment. The emphasis was on making me a better 'one-man band' rather than on helping me to become the effective leader of a strong orchestra.

Ultimately, however, the true leader needs to be equipped by God. Samuel Chadwick, the founder of Cliff College, wrote in 1932 that 'a ministry that is College-trained but not Spirit-filled works no miracles'.

In recent years it's been a great privilege for me to become part of the faculty of the International Leadership Institute, a role which has taken me to many parts of the world to train and to encourage emerging leaders. I'm committing a growing proportion of my time to the development of this new generation of Christian leaders, and I've been really encouraged to discover that God is giving his church some amazing visionaries, motivators and evangelists. He is equipping his church with leaders who are full to overflowing with the power of the Holy Spirit. I hope that I can prevent them from being turned into yet another generation of one-man bands.

Community

No one ever explained to me that the joy of being church is about the rich experience of belonging to a community. The Christian community is not only what's visible in the local church, it's the Christians whom you encounter in the unlikeliest places and among the most unusual people groups anywhere in the world.

Some of the most beautiful times of my life have occurred in encounters with this mysterious community of God's people. I have found it on Christian holidays, among mission teams, on pilgrimages, at conferences and in myriad short relationships, rich conversations and unlikely friendships. It's fascinating to watch younger Christians as they discover this community for themselves. It's intriguing to watch them as they discover just how wonderful it is. No one told me to look out for it, or encouraged me to connect with this, the most amazing network on earth.

Over the last few years I've travelled all over the world and have experienced the rich diversity of this global community for myself. I've laughed with sari-clad nuns in India, worshipped with African Christians in the bush, dreamt exciting new dreams with visionary young Americans, prayed with fervency alongside Christians from the persecuted church, and stood with expectant Hispanic Christians as the Holy Spirit poured down. These experiences have blessed me beyond words.

The writer of the Acts of the Apostles made it clear that the early church was a community in which everyone made their contribution. All the church members experienced a strong sense of belonging to, and responsibility for, each other.

> Every day they continued to meet together in the temple courts. They broke bread in their homes and ate together with glad and sincere hearts … (Acts 2:46).

Healthy communal life in a local church is a sign of God's presence. I believe that the communal life of the church is the antidote to family fragmentation and the breakdown of human relationships. It is God's healing answer to the lonely isolation in which countless millions live their lives. A healthy church celebrates the contribution which each and every one of its members can make.

Congregations which express God's Kingdom in such relationships are expressing his love. They are demonstrating that true worship flows from the richness of their communal life. Healthy churches enrich their people through networks of deep and caring relationships.

Churches must become centres of deep belonging. They must recognize that the world is not looking for an organization to join but a community to be part of. These communities don't refuse those who have no 'membership ticket' or 'certificate of baptism', but welcome all who are fellow travellers to join them on the road of faith. In fellowships like this, each one helps the others towards the goals of wholeness and holiness.

Post-modern society is not one mass culture but a celebration of many cultures. It does not consist of one kind of people, but of many different people groups. Life has not become more uniform but far more diverse, so there must be different kinds of church for different kinds of community. For the last ten years I've been part of a congregation dedicated to the arts. This artistic 'people group', with its richness of imagination, diversity of expression and commitment to creativity, has led to the development of a church where I felt my own gifts were valued and nourished. It's been a congregation where the Gospel has been made incarnate in a multitude of creative ways.

I was taught that the church was an 'all-age, all-purpose, all-embracing, all-culture' expression of God's Kingdom. No one told me that it was OK to belong to a cell church which gives space for distinctive kinds of people, and which encourages a multitude of different expressions of worship.

No one told me that God loves to see different groups enjoying the worship which most expresses who they are. I was never taught that even in the smallest kind of cell, where two or three come together in his name he is there with them.

The church must become a network of many cells. Some may meet on church premises or be drawn from different ethnic or socio-economic backgrounds. Some may meet in a tiny geographic area where two or three begin to form their own neighbourhood cell. Other cells may share a specific interest, background, workplace or experience. All different, yet all relating to the Body. These small cells must be free to demonstrate their different cultural identities. Many church leaders are unashamedly middle-class, and their theological training has separated them from the working-class culture of which they were once a part. As a result, genuine expressions of working-class culture are rarely found in mainstream church life. The cell church can at last break free from this monochrome identity.

Those who feel alienated from middle-class Christianity will be able to discover that their contribution is valued and affirmed. There must be room for those who prefer gut-reactions to concepts and who prefer worship that's more from the heart than from the mind. There must be cells for those who prefer rhythm to plainsong, and for those who understand feelings more easily than words.

I no longer want to be part of a bland, multicultural church which cuts out everything beyond middle-class normality. I'm excited about the growth of ethnic congregations which feel free to develop their own worship styles, to use their own language and to draw on their own cultural tradition. Christianity doesn't have to wear Western clothes. Ethnic cells need to function autonomously whilst being joined in regular fellowship with the wider Christian community.

No one told me when I was a young Christian that it was OK to start youth congregations. Young people don't need to wait to develop their leadership skills; they must be empowered to create their own styles of worship and be released into the gifts which God has evidently given them.

Young people must be given space to pray in their own language, sing to their own rhythm, affirm their own leaders and celebrate their own Gospel. These youth cells must be encouraged to develop their own initiatives for mission, explore their own styles of worship and work out their own response to the needs of the poor.

There is a wonderful richness in the diversity of cells meeting for worship. St Paul summed it up when he wrote, '... where the Spirit of the Lord is, there is freedom' (2 Cor. 3:17). Styles of worship are only the vehicles for praise. Some people are carried into the presence of God by noise and movement, others by silence and stillness. No one explained to me that the church must provide space for everyone to find their own community and their own expression of what it means to truly belong.

The church must become a place of many welcomes, where diverse people groups each find a place of their own in the family of God's people. The communal nature of church life is stressed in John 17, where Jesus prays for his followers that they may be 'one' – one with each other, and one with the disciples of all time. Luke's understanding of the early church was that it was a close community, united in a spiritual oneness. This oneness of heart is most clearly seen in the practice of holding 'all things in common' (Acts 2:44 and 4:32) so that there was not a needy person among them (Acts 4:34). No one explained to me that the church can be a network of small communities of people who belong to one another. No one gave me permission to be part of a church free to develop its own culturally appropriate worship styles, means of outreach, Christian education and mission. I long to see the establishment of a cell of committed Christians in every community, in every neighbourhood, embracing every class and condition of people. A kind of church where everyone can hear the Gospel and see it demonstrated among his own peer group and in his own language.

This multi-celled church may not be the kind of church which institutional Christianity would welcome, because it would be hard to control. God will recognize it, however, because it will carry the hallmarks of the Spirit. All this is so different from the kind of church I was introduced to in my early days of faith. That church was a uniform, middle-class community in which distinctives were frowned upon and people were expected to conform to one set of cultural norms. We all dressed the same, spoke the same and sang the same kind of hymns. No one introduced me to the multifaceted, multicultured, multidimensional kind of church which is emerging today. No one told me that church could be this colourful, artistic or visionary, or such fun!

Brokenness

Elsewhere I have described some of the hurtful experiences I have known in the life of the institutional church. But there have been others, too numerous to mention and too painful to describe, which still haunt me down the years.

No one warned me it would be like this. No one took me aside and explained that sometimes the people of

God don't act the way they should. I never conceived that people could be driven to say and do things by personal grievances, vendettas and jealousies rather than by the compassionate, all-forgiving love of God.

Like many Christian leaders, I've received my fair share of hate-mail; I've been the subject of verbose criticism (sometimes in public), and occasionally known a ferocity of division and anger between warring factions in the church which has shocked me to the core.

I was once invited to become senior leader of an evangelical church for three months after all the elders had resigned because their fellowship with one another had broken down. The church was left with no leaders and no constitution. It was a real revelation to me that sometimes things can go tragically wrong in churches outside the main denominational groupings. When I was a very 'green' young minister, I chaired a church council in which there was a blazing row about the distribution of the harvest gifts. I was fearful that something so trivial might even cause some of those present to come to blows.

Four years of ministerial training, a degree in theology, a working knowledge of New Testament Greek and a year of lectures on the Methodist rulebook never prepared me for this. It was my first experience in what was to become over twenty-five years of ministry in hurting churches.

If we're honest, many of us are living in a sea of pain in our local churches, whose waves are made manifest in a thousand different ways. They break over us in splits and secessions which are as predictable as the tide. They crash down on everyone when leaders fall and followers condemn. This sea of hurt rises when congregations treat their pastors with unkindness. It seeps through church life in gossip and false accusation.

Its powerful current forces people apart. It drives church councils to split and leaves many Christians drowning in unresolved conflict.

It was, to say the least, a bold concept. The leaders of the Baptist Union took their life in their hands by allowing anyone to say anything about the way that their churches were hurting in their annual conference, a meeting I was privileged to help to chair. And they didn't exclude themselves from any brickbats which might be thrown across the conference hall. It was, for me, one of the bravest pieces of Christian conference planning I've witnessed. There was something truly biblical about it. It showed a maturity of trust. It gave permission for anyone to say anything about the pain of being church in a time when most of us would rather gloss over our problems than look them in the face.

Throughout my life I don't think I've ever heard a group of local leaders talk so honestly about the pain of being church. Yet here, in this massive arena, people shared story after story of the pain of broken churches and fragmented fellowships.

It was refreshingly frank, and through the honesty there came a sense of relief. 'We're not the only church going through trouble … lots of others are suffering too.' Even in the process of sharing pain, there were bright rays of hope, and some were able to tell stories of reconciliation and a new beginning. It was a truly prophetic moment.

Unfortunately there are a lot of skeletons in a lot of closets in church vestries from one end of the country to the other. Perhaps it's time many others followed the example of the Baptists by giving people permission to take them out and bury them once and for all.

I believe that the task of mission is weakened in hundreds of churches because of unresolved conflict, ongoing tension, and the adoption of opposing positions over change and progress.

Relationships are not mended by pious prayers or by hiding unresolved arguments in skeleton-filled cupboards. Healing is a process, and reconciliation only comes when pain is identified and hurt is faced full-on. The journey of reconciliation demands courage and patience.

God loves us with an aching heart, like a jilted lover, waiting for his loved one to come back to him. He loves us with forgiving compassion, like a rejected father, waiting for his prodigal to return. He loves us with a spontaneous generosity, like a good man paying off his friend's debts without any hope of repayment. He cares for us like a generous stranger, giving the bond-price to let the slave go free.

Throughout his ministry Jesus modelled the Father's compassion for each of us. In his prayer in John 17 Jesus showed that he trusted his disciples. He was concerned about them. He prayed for their safety. He interceded for their unity. He claimed their protection. But most of all, he identified with them, for neither he nor they belonged to the world (v. 6-16). His love was encompassed in one supreme act of generosity on a cross and in his words, 'Greater love has no-one than this, that he lay down his life for his friends' (Jn. 15:13). If this Gospel of reconciliation and love is at the heart of our faith, we all need to learn how to live it with one another, too. I wish someone had warned me that church could be like this, and that only the love of Jesus can heal it.

Hope

All through my Christian life I've witnessed the slow decline of church membership in the UK. I've sat in endless committees and engaged in endless consultations about the decline of the church and the demise of the Christian 'institution'.

No one taught me that it's wrong to feel despondent about church statistics, or that it was sinful to imagine that the church had no hope and no future. I was never grounded in an understanding of the eternal nature of the church, a movement which has survived from distant history and which stretches towards an unshakeable eternity. If I'd really grasped the wonder of this, I think I'd have spent much less time worrying about the church and much more time just enjoying being a part of it.

I've become very irritated by the growing number of 'doom and gloom merchants' whom I seem to meet in all the usual ecclesiastical places. They pop up in church life whenever there is an enthusiastic young leader to be squashed or a dynamic vision to be quashed. And whenever they appear, they bring with them an air of depressing despair which drives the rest of us to desperation. I meet these doomers and gloomers at conferences of clergy, where they gather in clerical huddles and mutter about the dire future that awaits the denominational structures.

I meet them in musty vestries, sitting on church committees and conducting whispered conversations about the 'disappointing church membership returns' or the 'worrying trends in church accounts'.

I meet them in ecclesiastical organizations, as they reel from the dark news of the latest church statistics and look to forward planning with a seeming paralysis of fear.

So where is the risen Jesus in this prevalent school of doom and gloom theology? And where does resurrection fit into this churchmanship of death? And why do these people sound so credible when they are preaching a gospel without an empty tomb?

Several years ago, when I visited the beautiful Garden Tomb in Jerusalem, I joined the queue to walk into the dark little grave. An American tourist pushed in front of me (complete with baseball cap, cameras and Hawaiian T-shirt) and said to the guide at the entrance, 'I've only got a couple of minutes. What is there to see here?'

The guide (an ageing English clergyman) smiled, 'Don't waste your time looking in this tomb: he's not here, he's risen!'

It's time that the doomers and gloomers among us took a trip back to the empty tomb. It's time they discovered that, amazingly, 'He's not here, he's risen!' It's time they got hold of the message that with the risen Jesus around, there can be no place for doom and gloom. It just doesn't fit with a Jesus who always has the final victory.

Every one of us should be living in the joy, light and power of his Resurrection power every day of our lives. Christ's Resurrection has to be the greatest hope for the world and the surest certainty for the future of the church. And if you believe it, you must believe that his life is stronger than any negative force that would seek to overcome it.

There were three poignant symbols in evidence when they buried Jesus. There was the tomb itself, a symbol of death, mortality and human fragility: Jesus was dead and – in the eyes of the world – finished. There was the seal, a symbol of evil and corrupt authority, for his show trial had been manipulated by wicked men. There was the soldier, a symbol of the suffering, torture and pain to which he had been subjected. Yet on Easter morning he burst free. He left the tomb empty, for he had overcome the power of death. He broke the seal, for he had defeated the power of evil. The soldiers ran away, for he had overcome the power of suffering.

I can only guess that this event is considered irrelevant by the muttering, grumbling, depressive little brigade who often dominate church decision-making bodies. They don't seem to have grasped the true meaning of this most basic concept of the Christian story. Their pessimistic attitude denies the victorious Gospel which lies at the heart of true Christianity.

This resurrection life must be at the centre of our Christian experience. It should constantly infuse us with hope and brighten up our dullest days. It should lift our eyes above the struggles we face, to see the King whose victory we share.

When I was a teenager in Birmingham I used to hear stories of the great preacher in that city called Dr R.W. Dale. Once, when he was preparing his sermons for Easter Day, the truth of the Resurrection suddenly dawned on him. From that time on, whenever he conducted a service – even during Advent and Christmas – he always included at least one hymn which proclaimed the Resurrection message. He described this experience in his diary:

'Christ is alive', I said to myself: 'alive!' And then I paused: 'Alive!' And then I paused again: 'Alive!' Can that really be true? Living as really as I myself am? I got up and walked about repeating: 'Christ is living! Christ is living!' At first it seemed strange and hardly true, but at last it came upon me as a burst of sudden glory; yes, Christ is alive. It was to me a new discovery. I thought that all along I had believed it; but not until that moment did I feel sure about it. I then said, 'My people shall know it. I shall preach it again and again until they believe it as I do now.'

That's the answer! Whenever we come across the doom and gloom brigade in church life we must remind ourselves of the risen Jesus. In looking to him we know that our hope is assured.

My Jesus is looking for new leaders to build his church, new leaders to see his visions, new leaders to spread his Word in dynamic new ways. His Resurrection life has an unstoppable way of forging ahead, no matter how people may seek to stop it.

Movements quickly become institutions. Angry young visionaries can end up leading grey-headed hierarchies. Radical new ideas can suddenly look old-hat. Events that were once on the edge look tired and safe. Meanwhile, the emerging young leaders are kept standing in the wings. I hope they won't be kept waiting there for too long.

No matter what the future holds, broken bread and poured wine continue to be the focus of the church's hope, a sign of God's providential care, and a symbol that one day the journey will be over and his people will see him face to face.

No one told me that the joy of belonging to church is that we are the people who know the end of the story, who have read the last page of history and who declare the victory of Jesus. We are the people who live in the certainty of his coming Kingdom and anticipate the joy of meeting him face to face.

All the angels were standing around the throne and around the elders and the four living creatures. They fell down on their faces before the throne and worshipped

God, saying: 'Amen! Praise and glory and wisdom and thanks and honour and power and strength be to our God for ever and ever. Amen!' (Rev. 7:11-12).

No one ever told me that the future begins now; and the work of shaping what the church will be starts here. No one encouraged me to dream a dream, create a strategy and up roll my sleeves, for there is much to be done ...

5

What they didn't tell me about suffering

Real life

When I first set out on my Christian journey, no one warned me how I might react when I encountered suffering along the way. In the early days of my discipleship I never dreamt what a profound impact suffering could have on my faith. It would have been helpful if someone had warned me what to expect in those days of my naivety.

Life isn't easy, and there have been times when I've felt puzzled about the way in which things were turning out. There have been days when I have struggled to comprehend God's will and occasionally I have felt very angry with him.

My greatest struggles have often occurred when I have witnessed human suffering – and most especially when children have been involved. This first began over thirty years ago, when I went through a time of painful questioning soon after starting out as a minister in Yorkshire.

I remember taking a young family to a hospital near Leeds. In the back of the car, huddled in a blanket, was a frail three-year-old boy. He had been a bundle of energy just a few months before, but now he was weak and crippled with cancer.

He was nestling in his mother's arms. I saw his pale, drawn face in my driving mirror as we drove the weary miles to a special paediatric cancer unit. I feared that he wouldn't survive. His parents knew that the chemotherapy was putting an enormous strain on him and they didn't know where to turn for strength in their distress. As we waited outside the treatment room we sat in stony silence. The boy's father walked up the corridor and back, sat down, and walked off again. No words could console him. We watched the nurses come and go. Time stood still.

I could find no appropriate texts to quote, no theological statements to expound. Every argument I knew about 'the problem of pain' was silenced. I had nothing to say. But this was only the first time I struggled with suffering. As the years have gone by I have been 'silenced by life' again and again. No one warned me about this. Six years later, when I was a minister in London, my paper boy was knocked off his bike and dragged twenty yards under a car near my home. The drunken driver got off with only a minimum sentence. The boy's parents grieved with a depth of sorrow I had never encountered before. They sobbed for hours as they reeled in a state of inconsolable despair. All I could do was hold them and weep with them. There was nothing to be said, and the question 'Why?' hung heavy in the air.

They found some solace by making his room into a kind of shrine, spreading all the memorabilia of his childhood out on his bed. It became a permanent memorial to a life suddenly cut short. I felt that I had failed them. Years later, when I saw them again, their life was still freeze-framed at the moment of his death. Life had stopped the moment he was snatched from them. They never got beyond the question 'Why?'

A young teenager from my street disappeared one Saturday afternoon. He was last seen in McDonalds, and despite an extensive search involving hundreds of police, no one ever discovered what happened to him.

I shared the bewilderment of his broken family. They were in a state of such utter desperation that I feared for their sanity. Hours, days and weeks passed, until I prayed that, at least, God might show us where his body could be found. The mystery was never resolved. God seemed absent in their living nightmare. Why didn't he speak to us at such a time of unspeakable horror? Other situations from across the years flood into my memory. Some are too painful, even years later, to describe in detail. I remember comforting the parents of an innocent murder victim, visiting a bereaved family after the Dover ferry disaster, spending nights in hospital wards with those struggling for breath at the end of life. Times when the 'Why?' question was hammered deep into my psyche.

One sunny summer evening I sat beside a member of my church choir as he signed the permission form for relatively routine surgery. We were in a major teaching hospital, and the doctor was assuring him, 'This time tomorrow you'll be feeling much better.'

The next evening I was holding his hand as he struggled for life. His breathing was shallow as he was supported by a life-support system in the most hi-tech intensive care unit I've ever seen. Two nurses cared for him, and although he was completely paralysed they told me that he was still conscious. The only way he could show his distress was to sweat. In that living hell between life and death I tried to minister to him but I will never forget those dark hours of questioning. I prayed that the Lord would either heal him or release him. As I tried to sleep at night, the hiss and thud of the oxygen pump filled the air. His loved ones shared his strange existence between life and death until, at last, the doctor turned the switch and the life support hissed and stopped. The room fell silent. As my friend drifted away, I commended him to the God of all mystery. But the question 'Why?' remained.

Sometimes I have been unspeakably angry with God. Prayer has been suffocated by doubt. Life has been bleak and God has seemed distant, out of touch, absent. In some cases I was in a pastoral relationship with those who suffered and I was cast as the caring professional. On other occasions the crises were intensely personal, and I was emotionally involved in the trauma. Naturally, they were most difficult when they involved my own family.

How could I forget the night when Andrew, my three-week-old son, hung between life and death? How our GP came at midnight and warned that we should be prepared for the worst? His angry string of expletives on the phone when the ambulance service refused to come because they were on strike? Driving through London in a thick fog, an *A to Z* in my hand, and my wife and baby snuggled in the back seat, hanging on, and the desperate prayers I prayed that night? And once again, the question 'Why?'

No one and nothing prepared me for nights like that.

The question

Over the years, I've read a number of Christian theological and philosophical discourses on the subject of suffering. I've turned to them when I have been desperate for insights that might help me in my personal struggles, so that I, in turn, might help others in my pastoral work.

These books of apologetics for the faith have an important role to play. We need to understand the outcomes of the Fall and glimpse the mystery of God's gift of free will and the dreadful results of humanity's rebellion. It's important to understand that if there were no suffering, many beautiful things about the human spirit would be denied. It's right that we share the Resurrection hope of a new beginning, a second coming, a new Jerusalem, that we know for sure that a time is coming when every tear will be dried and death will be no more.

But these great Christian beliefs, good and profound as they are, never really helped me in the midst of the most desperate situations, when I was wrestling with the question 'Why?' Don't get me wrong: I support the need for an intellectual rationale, for theological apologetics, and for biblical insights in equipping us in the faith. But I couldn't handle them in the heat of a crisis.

Trite statements and throwaway comments like 'Every cloud has a silver living' always infuriated me at times like this. On 'Why, God?' days, Christian platitudes sounded shallow, and attempts to explain God's purposes through suffering seemed little short of blasphemous. There was usually no 'silver lining' to be seen beneath the clouds of despair.

In hard times like this I often went back to wise words spoken by my college principal, Howard Belben, who said to me, 'In my ministry, when I've come up against the question of suffering, I've never tried to avoid it, sublimate it or pretend it wasn't there. I always saw it like a train of thought that I couldn't quite resolve. So I shunted it into the sidings of my mind. And time and again across the years, when the question was less immediate and the situation less emotive, I've taken the question out of the siding to think about and to seek an answer. When I've been less emotionally engaged I found it easier to ask God "Why?" and to ponder. The big questions are always with me; they are part of me, part of my faith, and one day I'll know the answer. I haven't ever answered the question, but I think I've learnt how to live with it.'

Of all I've read and heard in Christian apologetics about this question, nothing has helped me more. I'm suspicious of those Christians who claim to have got the question sorted, for I honestly have to wonder if they've been to the places I've been, seen the things I've seen, and shared the moments of anguish that I've shared.

When I've spoken of my inner struggles with this issue, I've known Christians look at me as if I was letting the side down. Their looks have implied that my faith isn't victorious enough, my prayer not powerful enough, or my understanding profound enough. I beg to differ with this constantly victorious view of life, and I take my lead from Job, who said

> Then Job replied: 'Even today my complaint is bitter; his hand is heavy in spite of my groaning. If only I knew where to find him; if only I could go to his dwelling! I would state my case before him and fill my mouth with arguments. I would find out what he would answer me, and consider what he would say. Would he oppose me with great power? No, he would not press charges against me (Job 23:1-6).

Like Job, I've not tried to suppress the 'Why?' question in my own life. I've tried to bring it into the open in my relationship with God, for this is where it belongs. Like my college principal, I've brought this big question out of the sidings across the years, so that now it's a part of me and part of the depth of my believing.

But no one told me that it was OK to ask 'Why?'

Incarnation

My visit to a hospital in the centre of Croydon was an unusual one. I was visiting an older minister who was suffering from a rare blood disease. The prognosis wasn't good. As I entered the dull Victorian ward he shouted a friendly greeting and shuffled towards me in his bright red silk dressing gown. He was glad to see me, and I him.

You can't do a 'professional' visit with a fellow minister. They know the catchphrases and see through the courtesies. You have to be real. He told me that his time of illness had been a time of learning, and there was a lot that he wanted to share.

'In all my years as a hospital chaplain,' he confided, 'I never realized what it was like to be stuck in here. I used to breeze in and out and say nice things to people, but I was always on the outside looking in. But now, you see, I'm on the inside, too. I get woken up at some ungodly hour. I suffer those wretched transfusions. Like them, I don't know what the future holds – I'm just going through the mill like everyone else. Now, the other patients let me get close to them, and let me pray with them. I've done more as a patient here in a few weeks than in years of hospital chaplaincy.'

He saw his time in hospital as a parable of incarnation, for Jesus lives on the inside of suffering, too. The late Bishop David Shepherd, who devoted so much of his life to alleviating the suffering of the poor, once said,

'The incarnation meant truly entering into a world where there was indignation, corrupt authority, sickness, adultery, betrayal, agony and bloody sweat. If we believe that God is really incarnate, he is frighteningly close; he meets us where we are.'

Some years ago one of the real movers and shakers on the Christian scene was a leader called John Wimber. I loved his writing, and his vision for a different culture of church was way ahead of its time. All over the world, Vineyard churches sprang up, distinguished by a style of informality and welcome which was so much in keeping with the character of their founder. One night I managed to get a seat to hear him preach in London. The meeting was at Methodist Central Hall in Westminster and the 'house full' signs were out. After an inspiring time of worship the great man got up to preach, but he was only a shadow of the figure I'd seen at Spring Harvest some years before. Cancer of the throat had taken hold, and his voice was cracked and monotone. Every few seconds he had to spray saline solution into his mouth, for his saliva glands no longer functioned. My heart went out to him, but as he preached, that vast congregation was in rapt attention. They were literally clinging to his every word.

'Of all the experiences of my cancer treatment,' he said, 'none has been worse than going head first into the tunnel of the scanner. I suffer from claustrophobia, and the very thought of going in there was more than I could handle. But when they told me that during the radiation treatment I needed a protective mask covering my whole face except my throat, it was just too much to bear. I simply couldn't cope. But then I remembered the incarnation, and I remembered that, if I invited him, Jesus would come inside the mask and travel into the treatment room with me. That day, I discovered what incarnation really meant.'

Jesus loved the earth with a depth of compassion beyond our understanding. He leapt down from heaven to earth at enormous personal cost: a cost he paid to share our suffering on the inside. I wish I'd known the poignancy of this from the very beginning.

Jesus

Jesus was born in a borrowed stable and buried in a borrowed tomb. He was rejected by the people he grew up with and who had known him all his life. He was snubbed by the religious elite. He was betrayed and abandoned by his closest friends. They were the very people whom he might have expected to stay loyal to him in the darkest days. He was betrayed by one of his closest friends. Jesus knew what it was to be human – to struggle with temptation, to wrestle with the will of God, to agonize over the cost of total obedience to the Father. He knew the unfairness of a corrupt trial and the humiliation of mental and physical torture. The pain of the cross was as great as any pain we'll ever face. He even knew hell in that one bleak moment of separation from his Father.

There was no dark human experience he was not willing to go through as he made his painful pilgrimage to the cross. But as Jesus hung there, he entered into our suffering and became incarnate in the question 'Why?' When I first set out on the Christian journey, no one explained what a strength 'Emmanuel, God is with us' can be when words and explanations fail us. The heat has been taken out of my anger and the sting out of my questioning when I have known his immanence in the midst of terrible suffering itself.

On the day after Boxing Day 2004, I should have been on holiday in Devon. Instead I was at Premier Radio, trying to work out how to cover the Tsunami disaster. Of all the natural disasters of my lifetime nothing has ever seemed so real or horrific to me as this.

I interviewed church leaders and theologians, but they seemed at a loss for words. Like me, they were struggling with the big 'Why?' Even the Archbishop went on record as saying it made him question his faith. What horror, what grief, what suffering. 'Why, God, why?'

Some of my Christian friends appalled me. 'It's God's judgement. It's because we haven't lived just lives,' I heard them say. If this was their answer to the 'Why?' question, I wish they'd kept their mouths shut. Sometimes Christians can be such an embarrassment to the faith. Whenever this question looms large, Christians like this turn to the Old Testament with relish. 'Why the tsunami?' 'God's judgement on secularization,' they reply. 'Why Aids?' 'God's judgement on homosexuality,' as they rub their hands in anticipation. 'Why 9/11?' 'God's judgement on abortion,' as they point the accusing finger.

But they never seem to follow their own logic, pursue their own argument, or see this thinking through to its conclusion. Why was God's judgement on secularization poured out on some poor Indian woman, eking out a living as the wife of a humble fisherman? Why was his judgement on the gay community inflicted on some orphaned African child dying of Aids? Why was God's wrath about the sin of abortion vented on some Christian firefighter, trying to save lives at Ground Zero?

No. Think again. And, if you believe these things to be true, for goodness' sake keep silent. Your contribution does nothing but repel people from a faith like this, or a God like that.

In my own dark tsunami vigil, sitting in a tiny radio interview room in London's Victoria, I found a glimmer of light. I dialled a number in Sri Lanka and, to my amazement, got straight through. The line was clear; they could have been talking from the room next door.

'We were all in church,' the woman said in a perfect English accent, 'about a hundred of us, when the tsunami hit our village. The church is on a hill, and we saw the wave sweep in and take our village away. Thirty-eight of our neighbours were dead or missing when we came back down the hill. We walked four miles for water today, and there's no food yet. The roads are blocked, and everyone is living together in my brick house, the only house left in the village.'

As I listened intently to this horrific story, one person's experience out of millions, I suddenly heard the sound of singing. 'What's that?' I asked. 'That's the prayer meeting,' she replied. 'They're praising and praying outside my house.'

Whilst the great theologians of the world pondered 'Why?' and church leaders struggled for words, I could hear the sound of singing. Those traumatized people had discovered that even though the question remained, there was something stronger, more powerful: Christ was with them. He knew what it was to suffer, and he was walking beside them in their darkness. I still ask 'Why?' and sometimes I still ask it in anger. But now, thirty years on, I have a quiet assurance that whatever the answer might be, he is alongside. He's under the load, inside it all. The Christ who suffered and who suffers still is with me in the midst of suffering. But no one told me this.

The cross

I empathize with the spiritual journey of the poet W.H. Auden. He abandoned Christianity for many years while he explored the writings of people like Blake and Marx. But around 1939 he returned to Christianity, describing his journey as the gaining of a 'painfully slow intellectual grip on God'.

Auden's poem 'Friday's Child', written in memory of Dietrich Bonhoeffer, sums up this struggle. God is not to be found in the frantic disquisitions of philosophers but in the silence of the cross, a silence which still speaks today.

> Meanwhile, a silence on the cross,
> As dead as we will ever be,
> Speaks of some total gain or loss,
> And you and I are free.
>
> To guess from the insulted face
> Just what appearances he saves
> By suffering in a public place
> A death reserved for slaves.

This image of the cross has sustained me through my hardest days of questioning. When I'm really struggling, I hold on to my mental image of Jesus on a bloodstained cross, and hear again his words of dereliction, 'My God, my God, why?'

I wish that someone had told me at the very start of my faith journey that it was OK to be real with God in moments like this. I wish they'd warned me that God didn't really expect that when I was torn apart I should put a brave face on things, shout 'hallelujah', or recite ten good reasons why there should be suffering in the world. I wish someone had suggested that instead I might listen out for 'the silence of the cross'.

Dietrich Bonhoeffer, the eminent German church leader imprisoned in Tegel jail for his opposition to Hitler and the Nazi regime, wrote in one of his *Letters from Prison*

> God lets himself be pushed out of the world on to the cross. He is weak and powerless in the world, and that is precisely the way, the only way, in which he is with us and helps us. Matthew 8v17 ('he took our infirmities and bore our diseases') makes it quite clear that Christ helps us, not by virtue of his omnipotence, but by virtue of his weakness and suffering.

Stephen Plant, author of a scholarly book examining the ethics of Bonhoeffer's theology, concluded that

> God's silence on the cross is not a silence of indifference, despair or bewilderment: it is a silence of utter involvement and sheer passion. It is not an empty silence, for it addresses Christians in the Church community, in the commands of God and in the shaping of human character. In the silence of the cross God both takes responsibility for the world and gives responsibility to those prepared to serve it.

But why did no one tell me?

The call to suffer

One day Zebedee's wife came to ask Jesus if James and John could be promoted, 'one to sit on his right, and the other on his left'. She wanted them to occupy the positions of power in the coming Kingdom.

Her question revealed how little she understood about his teaching and how limited her knowledge was about the manner of his coming. Jesus turned to James and John, from whom the idea of 'promotion' had probably come, and asked, 'Can you drink the cup I am going to drink?' (Mt. 20:22). Jesus needed to make it clear that an implicit part of their call was their willingness to suffer for him.

When I first became a Christian, no one made it clear to me that this was part of the package. From the outset I heard great stories of the men and women of faith who had suffered and even died for Jesus, but I can't recall anyone telling me that I should realistically expect to suffer for Christ myself. It seemed to be news to James and John, too. Apparently James took up the challenge, because in Acts 12:2 we read that Herod had James the brother of John put to death by the sword. Historians believe that James was the first of the twelve to suffer martyrdom when he was killed in Jerusalem under the persecution instigated by Herod Agrippa.

One day my college principal asked me to look after a Macedonian minister who had come to study at our Manchester college for a year. It was my first direct contact with anyone who had been persecuted for their faith under Communism. I found his faith infectious.

Every day he struggled to master English, and every night he invited me to join him for his evening devotions. When he prayed last thing at night, he used his Macedonian vernacular. I didn't understand a word of it, except when I heard him speak my name and I knew that he was praying for me. At the end of the college year he invited a group of us to visit Macedonia with him. It was a very long and difficult journey in a twelve-year-old minibus, and when he invited us to take Bibles across the border it really brought his situation of Communist oppression home to us. The penalties for such an activity were severe, and I had never felt so scared in my life.

I will never forget the people we met in Macedonia nor the suffering which some of the ministers had endured for their faith. One senior minister had been in and out of prison many times. He gripped my hand and said, 'In the West the trees are lush and green. They stand tall and proud and close together. Here the trees stand alone, gnarled and weather-beaten, made strong by wind and weather. When the strong winds come the lush trees all collapse, but the gnarled old tree stands firm. Beware, for the Christians in the West have not endured as we have. And now they are not as strong.'

Times of persecution have sometimes been the mainspring for the renewal of the church and for powerful Christian witness. When I first became a Christian, I did not understand that suffering is integral to our calling and part of the way in which we celebrate Christ's life.

Two of my early missionary heroes were Jim Elliot and Nate Saint. They were Christian aviators with the Mission Aviation Fellowship who were pioneer missionaries among the Auca Indians. Their martyrdom, along with that of others from their team, took place on a river beach deep in the jungle. They were speared to death by suspicious tribesmen with whom they were trying to share the love of Christ. The story of their mission didn't end there, however, for Elliot's widow

Elizabeth and Nate's son Steve continued the work.
Elizabeth once wrote

> I have found it to be true that obedience may lead me
> to very unexpected and unspiritual situations – which
> are meant to teach me to be meek and lowly in heart.
> Sometimes the guidance of God can lead us into the
> wilderness – for that's where he took Jesus to be tempted
> for 40 days and nights. It could be the same for us.

I will never forget the scene at the Congress on
Evangelism held in Holland in 2000, when Steve Saint
stood on the platform and introduced the Christian
elders of the tribe his father had given his life to reach.
One of the men had been instrumental in his father's
death. The applause was so deafening that it must have
echoed to the heights of heaven. The Kingdom of God
had spread throughout an unreached people through
the blood of these young martyrs.

Some contemporary Christian books seem to imply
that suffering and sacrifice have little or nothing to
do with Christian lifestyle. They appear to teach that
Christianity is only about receiving forgiveness, joy,
peace, prosperity and heaven. There's no place for the
call to suffering.

Discipleship is marketed as a kind of cure-all, and
sometimes even as a short cut to prosperity. This
greed-focused spirituality finds no place for the 'cup of
suffering' and doesn't seem to recognize that suffering is
an integral part of following Jesus. Dietrich Bonhoeffer
once wrote

> Whoever wishes to take up the problem of a Christian
> ethic must ... from the outset discard as irrelevant the
> two questions which alone impel him to concern himself
> with the problem of ethics, 'How can I be good?' and

'How can I do good?', and instead of these he must ask the utterly and totally different question, 'What is the will of God?'

Bonhoeffer's insight is profound. Ultimately, we must all fulfil the will of God – whatever that may mean for our lives. Often, persecuted Christians don't seem to question their own suffering in the way that we do. They find comfort and joy in accepting it as part of God's will for them. They see it as a privilege and even as a blessing. Sometimes they even seem to feel sorry for us because we don't share in their blessing of persecution. This belief in the acceptance of God's will was no mere philosophical concept for Dietrich Bonhoeffer. One day he was transferred to Flossenburg concentration camp at Hitler's personal order. In one of his final conversations with a fellow prisoner, he said, 'This is the end – for me the beginning of life.'

He was tried at night, and at dawn ordered to undress. The SS camp doctor who was present to certify his death later stated that Bonhoeffer first knelt and prayed. At the gallows he prayed again before climbing the steps.

No one explained to me that this invitation to suffer is such an integral part of the Christian life. We do not follow one who came as a mighty emperor riding on a warhorse. His Kingdom was not about power, money or status. He came in the form of a servant. God become a baby, the King crucified as a common criminal. He came to suffer, and to invite us to obey the call to suffering.

Christ's topsy-turvy teaching sets all our human value systems on their head. His Kingdom was not about luxury and ease, but about service and sacrifice. No mighty stallion carried him into Jerusalem, but a donkey bore him up the road to death. His seamless garment was the winner's prize in a gambling game. The Man with everything was left with nothing. He came to suffer, and to invite us to share his life of suffering. In our willingness to suffer we celebrate his life, the life of the Suffering Servant.

Finish the race

One of the most remarkable people that I've come to know over recent years is Baroness Caroline Cox. Her commitment to religious freedom and to the needs of the persecuted church has been outstanding. A few days after the screening of the BBC *Everyman* documentary about her attempts to free slaves in Sudan, she told me about her friend Bishop Macram Max Gassis. In the western mountains the bishop, wearing his full ecclesiastical regalia, preached to his people in Sudan

> Christ is calling us, the people of Sudan, to the privilege of sharing his suffering, to be with him on the cross, and to bring reconciliation and redemption through this suffering. We have not asked for this fighting; it has been forced upon us. We can ask that the days of our suffering be shortened, but we cannot avoid the cross. God has helped us in our suffering. People from abroad are struck by our smiles and our serenity even while we are suffering.

Like Paul, Bishop Gassis had grasped the importance of 'finishing the race', no matter what the cost. This is true discipleship, but I fear that the cost of it has been greatly undersold. The church is reaping a barren harvest because of it. But the cost of discipleship isn't only to be paid by those who are persecuted in places like Sudan. There is a cost we all must pay.

At the end of my pilgrimage to Ephesus, the Turkish tour guide accompanied us to the airport. She seemed sad that she was soon to bid us all farewell. As the coach rumbled along the motorway, she whispered to me, 'I have one more surprise left: Miletus.'

This comment sent me scrambling for my Bible concordance. Miletus wasn't one of the seven churches of Asia. In fact, I'd never heard of it. But as I turned to Acts 20 I saw how poignant and important a place it was: it was where Paul said his last goodbye to the church leaders from Ephesus. Our coach pulled in beside the remains of a huge Roman fortress. The sea had long receded, and this once great port was now nothing but a crumbling ruin. Paul had arrived by sea to meet the Ephesian leaders here. He had already caused a riot in Ephesus and he didn't want to cause further problems for them, so he arranged this secret farewell meeting at Miletus.

The leaders from Ephesus were under great threat, and Paul also looked to his own future with a growing sense that suffering was imminent. The thirty pilgrims on my tour followed me past the ruined fort to the place where boats like Paul's would once have been moored. We ambled across the rough scrubland to a gnarled old tree where we stopped to say our goodbyes, to pray for one another and to end our pilgrim trail. There, in the shadow of the sprawling tree, as the midday sun scorched the ground all around, I read Paul's words.

And now, compelled by the Spirit, I am going to Jerusalem, not knowing what will happen to me there. I only know that in every city the Holy Spirit warns me that prison and hardships are facing me. However, I consider my life worth nothing to me, if only I may finish the race and complete the task the Lord Jesus has given me – the task of testifying to the gospel of God's grace. Now I know that none of you among whom I have gone about preaching the kingdom will ever see me again (Acts 20:22-25).

My group of pilgrims, black and white, old and young, poor and prosperous, shared the challenges which faced each one of them and prayed for one another. I was moved to tears. Some of them faced personal suffering back home: a suffering implicit in caring for someone who made enormous demands; a suffering caused by choosing a life of integrity, resulting in alienation at work; a suffering wrought by persisting with a difficult relationship when others would have discarded it; a suffering caused by forgiving even more than seventy times seven. In that moment, the experiences of our time in Turkey together were crystallized. In the footsteps of Paul we had discovered that suffering really is part of the discipleship deal for all of us, whatever our life back home. I left the shade of that old tree with a new commitment to follow Christ whatever the cost.

The 'why' of suffering

One Sunday morning, an elderly church member glared at me at the door. The annual Methodist Covenant service had just finished and we had renewed our 'Covenant with God', using John Wesley's famous Covenant prayer of commitment. As the old man gripped my hand I realized that this was a significant moment for him. He wasn't going to complain about my choice of worship songs or the microphone booming or the heating being on too low. It was something much more serious: 'Every year you use Wesley's prayer. It's rubbish. How can we possibly pray "Put me to doing, put me to suffering, let me be employed for you or laid aside for you"? What a stupid thing to pray.'

I went to see him the following week, and we talked further about the great mystery of suffering. A few months later the same man grew very sick. An industrial chemist throughout his working life, he had been exposed to many chemicals used in the manufacture of paint. He died an awful death, his skin so swollen and discoloured that he was barely recognizable at the end. He never did understand Wesley's prayer, though he died honourably and 'in the faith'. Perhaps in some mysterious way he did fulfil the Covenant prayer in his own life.

At about this time I wrote the following meditation:

The nurse went up a flight of stairs;
the hallway rang with noise.
The smell of disinfectant filled the air.
I turned into the ward
and looked along the row of beds,
and saw the face I knew.
The eyes were different now,
sullen,
sad,
and dry.
I could not speak.
No word was adequate.
I went and took the thin white hand in mine,
and touched the agony.
A jarring shock ran through my soul,
and time stood still.
I shrank away, defeated,
asking 'Why?'
I cannot understand.

> A picture fills my mind:
> a vivid picture of a bloodstained cross.
> A voice cries out through time,
> 'My God, my God, why?
> Lord Jesus, you have gone before;
> give me your strength,
> to shout through my confusion,
> thy will be done.'

I had tried to explain to him that our willingness to suffer was an aspect of obedience. We stand beside Job and say to God, 'OK, throw at me everything you've got, but I'll still go on trusting you.' We stand with Jesus in Gethsemane and say, 'Thy will be done.'

Pain

When suffering has crossed my path, time and again I've found myself turning back to C.S. Lewis's *The Problem of Pain*. For me, it is the benchmark against which all other books on this subject should be measured.

The Problem of Pain has an important role to play in helping Christians to face up to the big questions of their faith. It's certainly not light reading, as each chapter is a closely argued defence of the purposes of God. It's important to grasp the meaning of each section as it all builds towards an apologetic to answer some of the great 'why' questions of our faith.

In his preface Lewis makes it clear that he has never really known pain himself, and that he recognizes that his intention in writing the book is 'to solve the intellectual problem raised by suffering'. So it's to be read as an intellectual argument rather than a personal insight.

Lewis helps us to grasp something of the mystery of God's gift of free will. Without it we would have been little more than robots, but with it we have the power to rebel and to create outcomes which can have dire consequences for the whole of creation. He explores the complex argument that sometimes God's desire to act and humanity's desire to exercise free will are in direct conflict. In this way God may be seen as weak, though in fact in investing humanity with free will he is strong.

Lewis explains that many of us are looking for God to act like a beneficent grandfather who will solve all the world's ills. This easygoing attitude, however, is the kind of trait which leads to grandchildren being spoilt. It's not compatible with a God of love. There is a strength and sternness about love which is vastly different from 'kindness'. As Lewis puts it, 'God's love, far from being caused by goodness in the object, causes all the goodness which the object has, loving it first into existence and then into real, though derivative, loveability.'

But *The Problem of Pain*, good and profound as it is, was never much help to me in the midst of the most desperate pastoral situations which I've faced in my life and ministry. When I was in trauma, or facing the darkest hours of my own faith, the book didn't bring me much comfort. When I was personally wrestling with the question 'Why?' Lewis's classic apologetic for Christianity was far too clinical to speak to my need.

Even the most polished academic arguments never seemed appropriate when I was comforting the bereaved or at the bedside of someone who was in agony. On such occasions, any attempt to explain in detail God's purposes through suffering seemed little short of blasphemy.

I really enjoyed the movie *Shadowlands*, first screened in 1993. It's the story of what happened to C.S. Lewis some twenty years after he wrote *The Problem of Pain*. It tells the powerful story of this crusty old bachelor and his late-flowering love for Joy Davidman, an American poet. In the film Lewis is brilliantly played by Anthony Hopkins.

It portrayed Joy's agonizing battle with cancer and explored the problem of suffering from Lewis's very personal perspective. When Lewis married Joy in 1956, it was at first a marriage of friendship and convenience to enable her and her sons to get the necessary immigration papers to stay in Britain. By the time of her death from cancer three years later, however, their partnership had become one of passion, friendship and deep love. When Joy died, Lewis was paralysed by his loss. In the film we see how he was forced to wrestle with the 'Why?' question, not from a philosophical viewpoint as in *The Problem of Pain*, but as a man, as a lover and as a step-father.

After Joy's death, the movie shows Lewis and his stepson in the attic as they sort out the bric-a-brac from their life with Joy. After a poignant silence, Lewis asks the boy about his faith. Does he still believe? Tearfully and angrily, the child shakes his head and whispers, 'No.' Lewis pulls the lad towards him and simply says, 'That's OK. That's OK.'

Many of us face big struggles in our faith, similar to those depicted in the film. We have real questions about suffering and pain, about why God allows tragedies and disasters to occur in the world, about why our life turned out the way it did, about the loss of loved ones or the personal traumas which we face. At times like this we want to hear from someone who's been through the mill like us and who can speak as one who suffers rather than as a philosopher or academic.

This brings me to C.S. Lewis's second book on the subject of suffering. It's very different from *The Problem of Pain*. That was an academic masterpiece, but this later work is personal and intimate. It's not about an academic defence of the faith, but about the struggle of a Christian man who can't reconcile his experience of a loving God with the raw suffering of his life. Before his death, Lewis fell into despair and nearly lost his faith: *A Grief Observed* came out of that dark human experience of grief.

I came across this book by accident. I was discussing *A Grief Observed* by an author called N.W. Clerk with a friend of mine in Atlanta, when he turned to me and said, 'I'm sure that this book was written by C.S. Lewis himself.' I disagreed. There was no mention of it anywhere on the faded cover, but I thought I ought to check it out just to make sure.

Further research revealed that I was indeed wrong and that my American friend was right. C.S. Lewis was the real author of *A Grief Observed*. He wrote it in longhand in old notebooks after the death of his wife as a kind of therapeutic activity to get him through the pain of his loss. It was a book written to probe his 'mad midnight moments'. It questioned all that he had previously believed about life and death, about marriage and even about God. In his later book *Journal*, written three years prior to his death in 1963, Lewis explains why he wrote *A Grief Observed* under the pseudonym N.W. Clerk. He did it to protect some of his committed readers from his harrowing thinking and his agonizing questioning of the Christian faith.

I am glad that Lewis wrote *A Grief Observed*, and even more grateful that he was able to admit to writing it before he died. It takes us into the very eye of the storm, and shows us someone wrestling with God's will and able, ultimately, to cling on to faith.

The book takes the form of an undated journal in which Lewis documents with brief observations the overwhelming sensations of his grief, and then his confusion and rage at God. As time passes, he chronicles his return to faith and his acceptance of a new life. It is an insight into the powerful human experience of loss and the power of the presence of a missed loved one.

> But my heart and body are crying out, come back, come back. Be a circle, touching my circle on the plane of Nature. But I know this is impossible. I know that the thing I want is exactly the thing I can never get. The old life, the jokes, the drinks, the arguments, the lovemaking, the tiny, heartbreaking commonplace things. On any view whatever, to say, 'H. is dead,' is to say, 'All that is gone.' It is a part of the past. And the past is the past and that is what time means, and time itself is one more name for death, and Heaven itself is a state where 'the former things have passed away'.

Anyone who has been through theological college will know the kind of pressures which such an experience can bring. One might imagine that a theological college community might be a foretaste of heaven, but often the students are separated into theological camps which divide them from one another.

Malcolm Rothwell was in a different 'camp' to me, and because of that our ministries never connected. When I was researching my books on spirituality, thirty years after we were in college together, I came across his book *Journeying with God*. It was a remarkably frank and honest piece of writing. Malcolm's insights have challenged and nourished me in a way I never dreamt possible when we were students together so many years ago. The book describes his decision to take a thirty-day silent retreat with no television, radio, books or newspapers. He decided to eat alone, with conversation limited to one hour per day. Malcolm writes with compelling honesty, and it's clear that his retreat experiences really transformed him.

Earlier in this chapter I described some of my own angry questioning of God. I found it greatly reassuring that another Christian leader of my own generation, and coming from a different theological place than me, had known the same experience. He described what happened during the first week of his vigil:

> Towards the end of this first phase of the Exercises I began to feel a sense of anger welling up inside me. The reasons for this are not relevant, but I felt angry with God. It seemed to me that in part of my life he had let me down. I wanted some straight answers. In order to make this a fair fight with God I removed the large crucifix which was an aid to devotion during this first week, and the cushion on which it was placed and a small plant which was also in view. I did, however, light the candle. There I was, with God. Just the two of us. I began this hour of prayer by kneeling. God spoke. 'All you have to do is listen.' I refused point blank. I folded my arms in a gesture of defensive defiance. I was not going to listen. I looked for all sorts of distractions mental and physical. Eventually I felt impelled to open my arms. I heard a voice. 'There is no need to kneel, just sit, relax and listen. The first thing you have to do is put the crucifix back.' I refused. Again there was the gesture of defiance; the folded arms. This was a wrestling match to end all wrestling matches. I was not going to be bullied by God. After a long, long interval of time, I weakened. First the cushion went back, and then the crucifix and then the plant. 'No, don't put the plant at the side, put it at the foot of the cross.' I found

this to be quite overwhelming and totally unexpected. If I had thought about this beforehand would I have come to this conclusion? Would I have worked it out like this? I think not.

As I have wrestled with the great 'Why?' questions of my life and ministry, I've found Malcolm's experience very helpful. When we place life's traumas back at the foot of the cross, they become redeemable. It's as we place the big 'Why?' of life under the cross that we discover that the answer to it all lies right there, in that place alone.

It's as we put the troubling things of life into the context of his mysterious love, his self-giving sacrifice, his anguish and his desolation that we discover that 'the foolishness of God is wiser than man's wisdom, and the weakness of God is stronger than man's strength' (1 Cor. 1:25).

The challenge of suffering

Sometimes I have asked why God couldn't right the world's worst wrongs. Why couldn't he step in to stop man's inhumanity to man? Why, when some grain barns were full to overflowing, were people still starving? Why, when multi-billion-dollar pharmaceutical corporations had drugs for HIV and Aids, weren't they made available to the poor of Africa? Why have some asylum seekers been treated with such despicable callousness when justice was on their side?

This kind of suffering presents a challenge which none of us can refuse. Care for the poor and empathy with the suffering has to be the hallmark of genuine Christian spirituality. Mother Teresa's work in the slums of Calcutta flowed out of her faith in Christ and her relationship with God. My friend, a nurse called Fi Hibberts, was tending a skeletal dying man late one night when Mother Teresa pushed her closer to the patient. As she gripped the two of them together, she whispered, 'Love until it hurts.' Mother Teresa once said

> Our works of charity are only the fruit of God's love in us. That is why those who are most united with him love their neighbour most.

This is what Jesus meant when he taught us about the innate value of each and every human being. We are all created in the image of the Father. We are all priceless, precious, full of potential. Our true value rests in him, not in the labels which society sticks on us.

Recently I went to visit the office of Jim Wallis, one of America's contemporary Christian pioneers in caring for the poor. He and his team, based close to the White House in Washington, have continued to speak up for the oppressed and to develop practical deeds of compassion.

As I boarded the Washington metro train I imagined that I might be heading to a five-star US ministry complex. With their income from a popular magazine, a thriving website, a score of best-selling books and an international preaching ministry, I thought it might be like visiting a headquarters worthy of Microsoft.

The Jim Wallis team, however, called Sojourners, is based in a dangerous, run-down part of Washington where houses are boarded up, sullen youths sit on the walls beside the sidewalk and the wail of police sirens fills the air. Jim has chosen to base his thriving ministry in one of the neediest parts of the capital. On the day

I arrived, his latest book had made the *New York Times* best-seller list, but that same day he had been criticized by both the political right and the political left for his condemnation of self-centred politics. In *The Call to Conversion* Jim wrote

> The question we should ask is not what we should give to the poor but when we will stop taking from the poor. The poor are not our problem; we are their problem. The idea that there is enough for everyone to live at our standard of living, or that we are rich because of hard work and God's favour, or that poverty is due to the failure of the poor – all these are cruel myths devized by a system seeking to justify its theft from the poor.

The cost of speaking out for the suffering of the world can be great. If you stand with the weak, you must be prepared to lose your friends among the powerful. In *The Seven Deadly Sins* Kenneth Slack wrote

> There is a righteous anger which is an essential part of being human. The man who can look on cruelty and not be angry is not preserved in some sinless state of calm; he is defective in proper human emotion. Treachery, maltreatment of the weak, exploitation of the vulnerable, these and other acts ought to move us to anger. When we can look on them with Olympian calm we have not achieved an advanced staging post on the way to sinlessness, we have begun inwardly to wither as human beings.

Where people suffer in society, Christians have no option. We must speak out. We must seek justice. We must serve. We must care. We must love. For if we don't, the 'Why not?' question will surely come back to haunt us.

The invitation to suffering

Some of the most significant moments of my ministry have been spent in the company of those who suffer. I have known God's presence when comforting the bereaved, waiting with the dying, walking with the depressed, or listening to those who feel they've failed.

I have sensed the awesome presence of Jesus in these bleakest moments of human dereliction. I have seen the light of heaven break through the darkness and witnessed when God exchanged hope for despair. I follow a Saviour who sought out the suffering, who made himself available to them and who cared for them without limit. He offered compassion while the world hurried about its business, and he expects us to do the same for our generation.

When I first began to broadcast on Premier Radio, a frequent guest was an elderly nun called Sister Eva Hayman. Several years earlier, she had retired and gone to live in a convent in Wales. She was confident that her ministry was nearing its end and that God's call for her remaining years was to be focused on prayer.

After settling into her new 'retirement' regime she began to have a dream. It was recurrent and vivid in detail. She saw Jesus caring for a group of people, mainly men, who were evidently suffering. Many had scarred bodies and drawn faces. At the end of the dream Jesus turned to look at her, as if inviting her to join him.

The dream returned night after night. It so disturbed her that she shared it with her Mother Superior. The Mother paused. 'Have you ever thought of going to work among those with HIV/Aids in London?'

Sister Eva came out of retirement and pioneered a new ministry in the early days of that tragic pandemic. It was at a time when some Christians did little but pour scorn on those suffering, and point the accusing finger. Sister Eva followed the dream. Jesus was indeed looking for willing workers to get alongside those with HIV/Aids, to share their load and to suffer alongside them. In his earthly ministry Jesus poured out his life in healing and restoration whenever he encountered people who suffered. He recognized that human suffering is sometimes physical and sometimes mental. Sometimes it tears people apart through discordant emotions or spiritual confusion. Whatever the need, he sought to meet it.

Jesus invites us to partner with him in this ongoing work today. William Stringfellow once said

> A Christian looks like a sucker because he is free to give his life. To die – imminently – for the sake of anyone or anything at all – even for those or that which seem unworthy of his death, thereby celebrating the one who died for all, though none be worthy, not even one!

This kind of ministry is nothing new. Cyprian's gamblers were active in AD 252. They were not, as their name might imply, a group involved in roulette, poker or blackjack. They were Christian disciples who were willing to gamble with their lives in celebration of the One who gambled his. As the crowds fled Carthage to escape a horrific plague which was killing hundreds of their fellow citizens, Cyprian's gamblers were going against the flow. They were heading into the plague-ridden city to nurse the sick, to care for the dying and to bury the dead. This concept of 'gambling our lives for Jesus' has stayed with me down the years. I believe we need another team of Christian gamblers for our world today.

When the dreadful massacre in Dunblane occurred, I was at a loss to know how to cover it on my radio programme. The whole event was so sick and so devastating that almost any angle I chose seemed inappropriate. At last I plucked up courage to call Victim Support in the town. I felt that they, at least, might have a comment to make.

I was very nervous, fearing that I might be intruding at a critical time. A cheery lady answered, and after I'd explained who I was, she replied, 'Is that wee Robbie?' I responded 'Yes'.

'I came forward at one of your rallies,' she said, 'and I asked God what I could do for him in my town. He told me to set up a branch of Victim Support. And now I know why.' When the conversation ended I felt a surge of optimism. Right there in the midst of all that suffering was a disciple ready to care.

Time and again I have discovered people who have followed the dream. People who, often at great personal cost and sacrifice, have served others with humility and compassion. These are the unsung heroes of God's Kingdom. They know that compassion is crucial to discipleship and at the core of Christian believing. Os Guinness once said

> It is when Christians have at least partially entered into the profundity of identification that the Christian community has been at its most human and most sensitive and that its message has been most credible and compelling.

When I was visiting Manila for an international conference about Christian mission, I met a local minister working in the slums. He told me about his work and invited me to see first-hand what his church members were doing. I must admit that after all those hours in the conference, it was refreshing to get out and see something practical. The pastor took me to the nightclub quarter, and we walked down crowded streets filled with flashing neon and loud garish music. Nightclubs, strip joints and topless bars lined both sides of the street. Then he took me down dark alleys and past the red-lit windows of brothels. Prostitutes stood in the doorways inviting us in. I wondered where we were going.

At last he pushed open the door of a partly derelict building, and an elderly Filipina lady smiled at us as she held up an old oil lamp. She placed a finger to her lips and ordered, 'Shhh.'

As she lifted up the lamp and angled it to the room I gasped. There were children everywhere: on the table, under the table, under the sink, and covering every inch of the floor.

'Child prostitutes,' whispered the pastor. 'We give them food and safety. And every day the offer of a new life, away from here, when they feel they're ready.' He pulled the door shut and we were heading back towards the bright lights of Manila again. For weeks I was haunted by what I'd witnessed, and moved to know that here the people of Jesus were willing to take his love to a place of such deep darkness. It was a transformative moment for me. They, like countless Christians down the years and across the nations, had seen the dream. They had heard Christ's invitation to serve the suffering in his name. They were God's answer to the question 'Why?'

Beauty in suffering

During the years of my ministry I've seen the most beautiful things in the lives of those who suffer: a kind of beauty which defies logic; a selflessness that's not natural; a faith that simply radiates Christ's love. When someone is able to lay their suffering at the foot of the cross, God does something new with them. He transforms the tragedy into triumph and brings resurrection out of death.

When I see this kind of beauty in suffering, the 'Why?' question recedes and it's replaced by the question 'How?' How does Jesus manage to make something so bad so good? How does he turn something so awful into something so awesome? He transforms darkness into light.

I once came across a faded book on the bargain shelf of a charity bookshop. It's called *A Severe Mercy*, and it tells the heart-rending love story of Sheldon and his wife Davy Vanauken. It's the story of her tragic fight with cancer and her untimely death. What drew me to the book was the mention of C.S. Lewis on the cover. What was happening to the Vanaukens had also happened to C.S. Lewis as his wife Joy had struggled with the advance of cancer some time before. This is a book about two Christian couples trapped in impending tragedy, both struggling with the ultimate question 'Why, God?' Vanauken exchanged letters with Lewis throughout the months of his trauma. This correspondence, an important feature of *A Severe Mercy*, describes the struggle to make sense of suffering and to cope with intense and personal sorrow. It gives us another insight into C.S. Lewis's academic brilliance, personal tragedy and maturing faith in God. Here we see Lewis after he has survived the storm, ready and eager to help a Christian brother still passing through it. It makes powerful reading, and I was deeply moved when I read it. After Davy's death, Sheldon wrote

> One sleepless night, drawing on to morning, I was overwhelmed with a cosmos empty of God as well as of Davy. 'All right,' I muttered to myself. 'To hell with God. I'm not going to believe this damned rubbish any more. Lies, all lies. I've been had.' Up I sprang and rushed out to the country. This was the end of God. Ha!
>
> And then I found I could not reject God. I could not. I cannot explain this. One discovers one cannot move a boulder by trying with all one's strength to do it. I discovered – without any sudden influx of love or faith – that I could not reject Christianity. Why, I don't know. There it is. I could not. That was an end to it.

Sheldon's experience resonates with mine. Even in the darkest times, the bleakest days, the worst 'Why, God?' situations, I have found something holding me that was bigger than me. Even when I was mad with God and wanted to be rid of him, he still hung around, waiting. Again and again I have found myself coming back to those familiar words, 'Thy will be done.'

C.S. Lewis, writing to Sheldon Vanauken in *A Severe Mercy*, compared this agonizing process of growing into Christian maturity with the pains of childbirth. Lewis imagined what Vanauken's wife really wanted for him now.

> Do you imagine she herself can now have any greater care about you than that this spiritual maternity of yours should be patiently suffered and joyfully delivered?

Moments after writing this I turned on the television. The History Channel was revisiting the Aberfan disaster and interviewing the families of the many children who died in that small Welsh village. A mountain of colliery waste slid down onto the village school and more than a hundred children perished. It was a horrific disaster.

On the screen was the lined and grief-worn face of an old miner, and on the soundtrack a Welsh male voice choir was singing an old Sankey hymn about trusting Jesus. The camera moved in to a tight close-up as the old man, tears still filling his eyes, whispered in his lovely Welsh lilt, 'All I'd say is, if you've got faith in God, hang on to it. Hang on to it and never let it go. That's what we did. That's what saw us through. I don't know where we'd have been without it. That's what saw us through.' I knew what he meant. Here was a kind of human beauty made perfect through suffering. But why did no one tell me?

And so I reach my most recent experience of the big 'Why?' Anyone who has worked in an office context will understand how closely a director and his PA have to work together. God sent Camille to work with me nearly three years ago, and from the outset she was a personal assistant of the highest calibre. She organized me in the most charming way, answered my mail, booked my tickets, and kept me in touch with fifteen or more projects as I rushed around the world.

When Cam got cancer it knocked our office sideways. When the prognosis was poor, and the treatment awful and the uncertainty oppressive, there were times when all of us who worked with her felt deeply disturbed by the suffering we witnessed.

Cam is more than twenty years younger than me, happily married, and with the kind of faith in Jesus which lights up the room. As we walked that road with her we saw a rock-hard kind of believing that amazed us.

When the time came for our annual convention, Easter People, she wasn't well enough to travel from site to site with the core team, and her weakness from the chemo made her drawn and waif-like. She never stopped smiling, even through her tears.

On the last night of the event, in the packed Torquay Riviera centre, she gave her testimony. Hundreds hung on her every word. Her theme was 'For me to live is Christ, to die is gain.'

At the end of her testimony she invited any who faced cancer, or whose loved ones were suffering, to join her at the side of the hall so that she could pray for them. Scores of people from all over the auditorium filed down to join her. I was dumbfounded. I had hoped that at the end of her story we might pray for her, but her plan was to pray for others. I've seen in her a willingness to hold on to God for healing through thick and thin, whilst also being open to the possibility of suffering and death. As I write, her cancer is in a remarkable remission, and it seems that our prayers have been miraculously answered. A few months ago, however, the days were dark and the 'Why?' question hung over us like a cloud.

Perhaps Paul's statement, 'For me to live is Christ, to die is gain', encapsulates how we should all face up to the big 'why's' of life. Perhaps when we discover a joyful submission to his plans we enter into a peace which the world can only dream about.

There is a beauty in suffering. It shines from the eyes of those who have known the pain, faced the loss, lived the anguish and suffered the heartache. It flows from a spirit at rest in God, a heart at peace, even in the biggest storms of life. No one told me to look out for it, and I could so easily have missed what God can do because of it.

Epilogue

The stages of faith

Writing this book has had a cathartic effect on me. Some of the material was new, whilst other sections were reworked articles from across the years. All of it, however, was intensely personal and contained thoughts and ideas that I have found it important to work with and helpful to get onto paper.

As I was writing the final draft, I visited Emory University in the United States and was introduced to the work of James W. Fowler, a former professor at Candler Seminary, which is part of that university, and author of the classic work *Stages of Faith*.

As I travelled home on a long plane journey, I began to turn the pages of Fowler's landmark research. It's about the psychology of human development and the quest for meaning. As I read, I began to look at all that I had written in these pages from a different perspective. On that long dark flight I shared a bit of Fowler's own experience, when one sleepless night he faced the reality of who he really was:

> In that moment of unprecedented aloneness experienced in my thirty-third year, I found myself staring into the abyss of mystery that surrounds our lives. As never before, I found myself asking, 'When all these persons and relations and projects that shape and fill my life are

removed, who or what is left? ... During those moments I was not in my faith. I seemed to stand completely naked – a soul without body, raiment, relationships or rules. A soul alone with – with what? With whom?'

Of all the things I wasn't taught, this was perhaps the most significant. I was never taught that maturity as a Christian comes when I am able to move beyond those simplistic parcels of believing and begin to grasp something of the enormity of the Beyond, the Mystery of God, the Infinity of Eternity. I was never taught that maturity as a Christian is about being able to hold in tension the simplicity and complexity of faith. I was never helped to live in the tension between the joy of believing and the anguish of obedience. I was never instructed how to pray, even in the struggle of doubt. No one helped me to stand firmly in the paradox of a God who loves but who also judges, or to continue to believe, even when my faith was low. I found Fowler's insights so helpful. He wrote

> Faith is a coat against this nakedness. We all at certain times call upon faith to provide nerve to stand in the abyss – naked, stripped of life supports, trusting only in the being, the mercy and the power of the other in the darkness.

Fowler's work draws on the thinking of eminent psychologists and theologians. He and his students conducted endless case studies to illustrate his theories and he tested them in the highest courts of academic scholarship.

He concluded that for many of us, there are 'stages of faith'. He uses the term 'Infancy' to refer to undifferentiated faith, when we discover mutuality and trust. He talks of Early Childhood as an era of imagination and the formation of images of the numinous. He describes Childhood as a time for the forming of stories of faith, and Adolescence as an age for the shaping of a personal faith. Adulthood, however, is when paradox, depth and responsibility for the world come to the forefront.

As I have wrestled with Fowler's theory of the 'stages of faith' I've wondered if in fact I should retitle this book 'Five things I wasn't ready to hear when I first became a Christian,' or even, 'Five things I was told, but never heard when I became a Christian.' For perhaps what I've explored in these pages is something that only comes with adulthood and psychological maturity. Perhaps I have at last reached stage five in Fowler's definition. He wrote

> Unusual before mid life, stage five knows the sacrament of defeat and the reality of irrevocable commitments and acts. Alive to paradox and the truth in apparent contradictions, this stage strives to unify opposites in mind and experience. It generates and maintains vulnerability to the strange truths of those who are 'other'. And with the seriousness that can arise when life is more than half over, this stage is ready to spend and be spent for the cause of conserving and cultivating the possibility of others' generating identity and meaning.

No one told me that there are stages of faith, and that what I couldn't handle at stage one God gives me the grace to understand at stage five. No one told me that Christianity isn't all received in one handy package, but that it grows all the richer and more meaningful in the years of living and the decades of Christian experience. It is, indeed, a faith for life, for it addresses every stage of our development and brings rich meaning to every chapter of our journey.

The Judgement

In my early years as a Christian no one told me about the Judgement. In my denomination, judgement was an unspoken word, a biblical principle long buried by liberal tradition. As the years have gone by, however, I've become more and more aware of God's impending judgement on my life, ministry and work.

We have become a society preoccupied with how we score, and we rate our success or failure according to how many percentage points we improve by in our chosen field of work. Everyone seems preoccupied with the 'bottom line'. In accountancy terms, that's the number left at the bottom of the page when outgoings are subtracted from income: the profit margin. The bottom line for many teachers is how many students passed the tests that make up the educational league tables. The bottom line in medicine is how many patients remain on the waiting list. In retailing it's how many units were sold last month. In a legal practice it's how many cases were won; in policing how many crimes were cleared up; in the media how many viewers were watching.

But there's another bottom line. It's the bottom line of how we perceive ourselves. It's how we measure ourselves against our peers. Am I a success or a failure? Have I done well, or could I do better? Am I popular or invisible? Even more important is the bottom line of God's judgement on how we've lived.

Around my fiftieth birthday I went through a kind of mid-life crisis and began to wonder about the 'bottom line' of my life. To be honest, I sometimes feel a bit of a failure. In this world's terms I really haven't 'made it' big-time. I guess there comes an age in all of our lives when you have to face the fact that you haven't done all you'd hoped for, or found the success that others have seemingly achieved so effortlessly. I sense there are a lot of us around: people who would be glad of a taste of fame, even for fifteen minutes. Yet we live our days making the best of what we've got and learning to accept who we've become. Perhaps this feeling's accentuated in mid-life, when the track ahead seems shorter than the track already travelled.

The stark truth is that many mountains you once dreamed of climbing remain unscaled, and many ambitions remain unfulfilled. I see the popular heroes of our age paraded before me on TV screens and magazine covers across the world and try to exorcize my feelings of jealousy and to focus on what's really important. Again and again across the years of my discipleship I've become aware of what this is: God's bottom line. For, indisputably, he has one. God has his own ways of measuring success or failure. And I suspect that his league tables are rather different from our own.

In my more reflective moments I can sense him measuring my life. My plans might seem exciting to me, but they're useless unless they're given his nod of approval. My performance might seem outstanding to me, but it's hollow if my motives are wrong. My management might seem tightly efficient to me, but it's flawed if it isn't fully accountable to him.

So if I want to meet God's bottom line, I find that I must regularly place my 'doing' in accountability to his 'being'. God's bottom line isn't about profit and loss. It's about right and wrong, love and hate, good and bad, truth and falsehood, integrity and double-dealing. God's bottom line isn't measured by success. It's about obedience and faithfulness, and living a life given over to him. There is a bottom line more precious than ISAs, gilts, pension funds and deposit accounts. It's something called wisdom. And it's something that lifts my eyes above the glitter of a success-dominated society. It's only his wisdom that can help me avoid evil, guard my soul, live humbly, trust him, discern right, speak intelligently … and recognize that there's more to life than worldly success.

God's bottom line will be revealed when I stand before Jesus at the end of time and look into his eyes. Sometimes, in my honest moments, I look towards my personal judgement day and see so many opportunities for kindness lost for good: So many chances to show love missed along the way: So many hurting people who remained ignored: So many deeds that would have made lives different left undone.

No one warned me that out of all life's priorities I could overlook the most important of all. That I could forget to be merciful, compassionate, gracious and kind. To do the very things which would survive the fire of Judgement Day. Perhaps, in the theological gamesmanship I've played, I've missed the potency of this simple truth. Perhaps, while I was fixing my life on winning the world, I overlooked mercy and was in danger of losing my own soul.

Mercy is the hallmark of the Kingdom people, the characteristic of those who really belong. Mercy is the guarantee of human authenticity, the sign of the living presence of God. 'Blessed are the merciful, for they will be shown mercy' (Mt. 5:7).

John the Baptist condemned those who queued up on the riverbank to be baptized but whose lives did not measure up to the high standard of God's calling. He compared the religious hypocrites of his day to a 'brood of vipers' (Lk. 3:7), and was sarcastic about their claims to God's special favour just because they were the descendants of Abraham. (God could make more children of Abraham out of a pile of stones!)

John's ministry was a preparation for the arrival of Jesus. He believed that the best way of preparing the people for the coming Messiah was to call them to repentance and personal preparation.

No matter how uncomfortable we may find it, there is no escaping the fact that the teaching of Jesus is littered with powerful images of judgement. His whole ministry was a warning to us that one day we must face him as our Judge.

In the parable of the wheat and the tares we are told that both are to be allowed to grow together until the harvest. When harvest-time comes, the owner will tell the harvest workers to collect the weeds first and tie them in bundles, ready to be burned (Mt. 13:24-30).

In the parable of the servant who owed the king ten thousand talents, we learn that the king is merciful and forgives him the debt. But later, the same servant refused to forgive someone who owed him a measly hundred denarii. As a result, the king recalled him and handed him over to the jailers, to be held until he should repay his huge loan in full (Mt. 18:21-35).

In the parable of the sheep and goats, the peoples of the world are divided into two groups. Those who have ministered to the Stranger in his hunger, thirst, loneliness, deprivation, sickness and imprisonment are led to one side, and those who refused to offer help and service to the other. Those who have failed in their duty 'will go to eternal punishment' (Mt. 25:31-46).

Those of us who have only ever been taught to think of Jesus as our Friend, Saviour, Comforter and Guide would do well to recognize that he is also our Judge: today, and tomorrow; now, and in eternity.

In my early years of Christian discipleship no one told me that one of the greatest priorities of my Christian life must be to make time for confession, for repentance, and for saying sorry. I was not taught to live with a proper sense of the reality of judgement or an awesome enough respect for the ultimate purposes of God. Had I been mentored in this, I think my life and ministry would have been all the richer.

I was introduced to a kind of Christianity which was based more on my needs than on God's, a form of Christian humanism that missed out a true understanding of the awesome divinity of God. My understanding of God made him more like a pal and less like the Creator and Sustainer of the Universe.

Perhaps all five of the things 'I'd Wished I'd Known' would have come more easily to me if I'd started out with a greater sense of the power and majesty of God. I pray that I might know more and more of that in the coming stages of my faith. For, one day, I hope to live for ever in the fullness of His glory and to be enfolded in His Perfect Love. Until that day comes I continue to pray ...

Lord, I'm preoccupied with time:
Show me your omniscience.
I'm preoccupied with my busyness:
Show me your wisdom.
I'm preoccupied with fading things:
Show me your permanence.
I'm preoccupied with passing days:
Show me immortality.
I'm preoccupied with future plans:
Show me your great design.